DAVANTE ADAMS:

Redefining Receiver Dominance

Donald A. Bower

Davante Adams

Davante Adams

TABLE OF CONTENTS

Davante Adams

INTRODUCTION

Through the life and career of one of the NFL's most extraordinary players, "Davante Adams: Redefining Receiver Dominance" takes readers on an exciting trip. We dig into the incredible life of Davante Adams in this engrossing biography, following his ascent from impoverished origins to becoming a great football force to be reckoned with.

Adams' commitment to his profession and persistent will to succeed is clear throughout his career, from his early days polishing his abilities on the streets of Palo Alto, California, to his outstanding university career at Fresno State. From the difficulties he conquered to the mentors who helped him along the way, the book examines the crucial occasions that defined his journey.

Davante Adams

Adams' extraordinary effect as a wide receiver for the Green Bay Packers is at the center of this story. He has changed the art of receiver play with a blend of speed, agility, and an inherent understanding of the game. Exciting anecdotes of his outstanding performances, record-breaking accomplishments, and the close bond he has with his quarterback, Aaron Rodgers, bring the book's pages to life.

However, "Davante Adams: Redefining Receiver Dominance" is more than just a tribute to his achievements on the field. It explores Adams's personality off the field and creates a striking portrayal of the man wearing the helmet. Readers learn about his commitment to the community, his moral principles, and the difficulties he encounters while juggling the demands of a professional sports career.

This book gives readers a thorough knowledge of what distinguishes Davante Adams through thoroughly researched tales, exclusive interviews, and professional analysis. It captures the essence of his journey as he

Davante Adams

pursues perfection, faces hardship, and makes an enduring impression on the football world.

"Davante Adams: Redefining Receiver Dominance" presents an uplifting and captivating narrative that will stay with you long beyond the last page, whether you're a die-hard football fan, a reader of inspiring human stories, or just someone who admires the quest for greatness.

CHAPTER 1: WHO IS DAVANTE ADAMS?

A notable contribution to the National Football League (NFL) has been made by professional American football player Davante Adams. Adams, who was born in Redwood City, California, on December 24, 1992, has been renowned as one of the top wide receivers in the league. His rise among football enthusiasts from his early days to becoming a household name is a testimonial to his extraordinary talent and work ethic.

Adams' football career began while he was a student at Palo Alto High School in Palo Alto, California. His outstanding athleticism and on-field abilities during his high school years led to him being identified as a top football prospect. At Fresno State University, where he played collegiate football for the Bulldogs, he continued to develop his technique. Impressive performances

Davante Adams

during his undergraduate career demonstrated his capacity to make significant plays and grab passes in crucial situations.

Davante Adams was taken by the Green Bay Packers with the 53rd overall pick in the second round of the 2014 NFL Draft. His professional career officially began at that point, and he rapidly established himself on the field. Adams became a go-to target for Packers quarterback Aaron Rodgers due to his excellent ability to make contested catches, solid hands, and ability to execute precise routes.

Davante Adams has repeatedly shown to be a dominant wide receiver throughout his NFL career. Because of his speed, agility, and football IQ, he has been successful in several roles within the offensive schemes used by the Packers. He has developed a reputation for his propensity for making challenging receptions, frequently in tight coverage scenarios, and his capacity to get away from opponents.

Davante Adams

The stats and achievements of Adams speak loudly about his contribution to the field. He consistently has one of the highest receiving yards, receptions, and touchdown totals in the league. He and Aaron Rodgers' relationship has produced several memorable plays and game-winning moments.

Davante Adams is renowned for his humility, commitment, and hard work ethic off the field. He has participated in numerous charitable endeavors and neighborhood projects, exhibiting his dedication to giving back to the community that helps him.

Davante Adams, one of the most well-known players in professional football and a multiple-time Pro Bowler, is constantly redefining what it means to be a dominant wide receiver in the modern NFL. His transformation from a focused young athlete to a star player is an amazing tale that appeals to football enthusiasts and others who value inspiration from perseverance and success.

1.1: Early life and background

On December 24, 1992, in Redwood City, California, Davante Adams was born. He was raised in East Palo Alto, an area renowned for its difficulties and economic inequalities. Despite the challenges he faced, Adams was determined to overcome them and follow his passion for football. This tenacity was evident in Adams' early life.

Adams' relatives introduced him to the activity when he was a child. His father, Douglas Adams, Sr., coached minor football teams, and his older brother, Fred, was a college football player. Davante's passion for and talent for football was greatly influenced by his family's involvement in the game from an early age.

Adams went to Palo Alto High School, where he first displayed his football talent. Despite his outstanding performances, college recruiters originally paid him little attention because of his small size and the relative obscurity of his high school's football department. Adams, however, attracted coaches' notice with his tenacity and work ethic, which ultimately resulted in college scholarship offers.

He decided to play college football with the Bulldogs at Fresno State University. A turning moment in his football career occurred while he was a student at Fresno State. He rapidly attracted the interest of scouts and fans alike by establishing himself as a force to be reckoned with on the field. Adams's stats and highlight-reel exploits throughout his sophomore and junior seasons cemented his standing as a creative player.

A turning point in Adams' path came when he was selected to join the 2014 NFL Draft following his redshirt sophomore season. He decided to skip his final year of eligibility for college to chase his NFL goal. He made this choice because he was confident in his skills and determined to succeed at the highest level of the sport.

He surely developed his resiliency and unrelenting determination as a result of the hardships and trials he encountered during his upbringing. His upbringing in East Palo Alto, a town with its share of challenges, probably contributed to his will to succeed and overcome challenges on and off the field.

The early years and upbringing of Davante Adams provide an illuminating backdrop to his illustrious football career. His transformation from a young boy in a rough neighborhood to a renowned NFL star exemplifies the strength of tenacity, desire, and encouragement of those who saw potential in him.

1.2: Overview of football career

The football career of Davante Adams is evidence of his extraordinary talent, perseverance, and devotion to the game. His career has been filled with memorable experiences and outstanding accomplishments, from his early playing days through his rise to stardom in the NFL.

Davante Adams

College Football Career: When Adams joined the Fresno State Bulldogs, his football career took a huge step forward. In the two seasons he spent with the Bulldogs (2012–2013), he made an everlasting impression on the collegiate football landscape. He demonstrated his adaptability, quickness, and capacity for critical plays. Adams broke school and conference records in his second season with an incredible 131 grabs, 1,719 receiving yards, and 24 touchdowns.

His exceptional play at Fresno State earned him accolades as a unanimous All-American and a spot in the final four of the renowned Biletnikoff Award, which recognizes the greatest college football receiver in the country.

NFL Entry: After his redshirt sophomore season, Davante Adams declared for the NFL Draft. He was chosen by the Green Bay Packers with the 53rd overall pick in the second round of the 2014 NFL Draft. His professional career and entrance into the NFL were both launched at this point.

Davante Adams

Adams soon established himself as a major contributor to the Green Bay Packers. He established a solid rapport with veteran quarterback Aaron Rodgers and turned into a dependable target for him. He was a crucial component of the Packers' offense with his accurate route-running, capacity for contested catches, and aptitude for scoring.

Adams's numbers persisted in being impressive over time. In terms of receptions, receiving yards, and touchdowns, he consistently rated among the top wide receivers in the league. He became a go-to target for important third-down conversions and red-zone opportunities thanks to his exceptional catch radius and athleticism.

The success of the Packers, particularly their playoff campaigns and Super Bowl aspirations, was greatly aided by Adams' services. Fans, experts, and teammates all praised him highly for his on-field performances.

Football player Davante Adams has received a lot of recognition for his accomplishments. He was repeatedly chosen for the Pro Bowl, confirming his position as one of the best wide receivers in the NFL. His exceptional ability to consistently come up with pivotal plays won him the admiration of his rivals and cemented his status as a fan favorite.

Adams also broke numerous records throughout his career. He shattered the single-season and receiving touchdown marks for the Green Bay Packers, further solidifying his place in the annals of the illustrious team.

Football player Adams's career is the epitome of talent, perseverance, and fortitude. His career is an example for aspiring athletes of the benefits of steadfast attention to one's skill, from his record-setting collegiate receiving days to his dramatic and game-changing exploits in the NFL.

CHAPTER 2: GROWING UP AND DISCOVERING FOOTBALL

The biography of Davante Adams, from his upbringing to his discovery of football, is one of passion, tenacity, and the transforming influence of sports on young people.

Early Years and Family Influence: Adams was raised in East Palo Alto, a neighborhood known for its difficulties and socioeconomic inequalities. Redwood City, California, is where he was born.He was fortunate to have a family who supported and encouraged his hobbies despite the challenging situation. His father, Douglas Adams, Sr., was actively involved in coaching minor football teams, and his older brother, Fred, was a college

Davante Adams

football player. The fact that his family participated in football helped Davante develop a passion for the game.

Football Overview: Davante Adams first became aware of football through his family. He began perfecting his skills and establishing his enthusiasm for the game while playing with his brother and pals on the streets of East Palo Alto. He gained an understanding of the principles and the enjoyment of competition thanks to his early informal training.

Years at High School: Adams' love of football grew as he enrolled in Palo Alto High School. He stuck to his dreams despite the obstacles his neighborhood presented. Coaches and other players took notice of him right away because of his talent and work ethic. He displayed his innate athleticism and distinguished himself as a promising young athlete during his time in high school.

College Football at Fresno State: Adams' skill was honed when he attended Fresno State University. In his football career, his time at the institution was a turning point.

Davante Adams

Along with dominating on the field, he also gained a deeper comprehension of the nuances of the sport. He attracted attention and praise for his exceptional speed, agility, and flair for making plays.

Finding His Calling: As Adams advanced in football, he realized that the game wasn't just a hobby for him; it was his calling. His drive to succeed was strengthened by the difficulties he encountered as a child in East Palo Alto and the companionship he encountered on the field. He found that playing football helped him overcome his circumstances, set objectives, and work relentlessly to attain them.

The development of Davante Adams from childhood to football discovery exemplifies the transformational impact of sports. His journey from playing pickup games on the streets to becoming a star athlete at Fresno State is proof of the good effects of enthusiasm, tenacity, and the encouragement of a caring community. His path also serves as a testament to how important family and mentors are in fostering young people's aspirations and assisting them in reaching their greatest potential.

2.1: Childhood and Family Influences

Childhood experiences and familial influences had a big impact on Davante Adams's morals, character, and passion for football. Adams encountered difficulties as a child while growing up in East Palo Alto, California, which helped him build his resiliency and willpower.

Upbringing: East Palo Alto was renowned for its social problems and economic inequalities. Despite the hardships he faced, Adams was raised with a strong sense of family and community. These early encounters gave him the motivation to overcome challenges and pursue success.

Adams was fortunate to have a family who encouraged him to pursue his goals. His father, Douglas Adams Sr., coached juvenile football teams, while his older brother, Fred, played football. His love of football was sparked by early exposure to the game and the influence of his family. His journey was built on their unshakeable faith in his potential.

Learning Values: Adams began to develop the virtues of self-control, perseverance, and determination at a young age. His upbringing in a setting that valued resiliency and tenacity, as well as his family's engagement in football, served to further solidify these qualities.

Football as a Positive Outlet: For Adams, football evolved into something more than just a sport. He found a way to focus his energy and drive through the camaraderie he felt on the field and the concentration needed to succeed in the sport. A road out of potentially harmful influences and toward a bright future was provided through football.

Using Adversity as Strength: Adams' character was formed by his difficult upbringing. The difficulties he encountered strengthened his resolve to build a better life for himself. He took this fortitude with him on the football field, where he applied his life lessons to an unwavering work ethic and a desire to win.

Family Tradition: Adams felt inspired and motivated by the football tradition in his family and by the participation of his brother in the game. It demonstrated the opportunities that football may present and inspired him to obstinately pursue his love.

To sum up, Davante Adams' football career was founded on the foundation of his upbringing and familial influences. He became the tenacious and motivated person he is now as a result of the difficulties he overcame and the encouragement and values established by his family. His exceptional football career and his dedication to having a positive influence both on and off the field were both shaped by these early events.

2.2: Initial interest in sports

Davante Adams' early enthusiasm for athletics was sparked by his inherent athleticism, competitive nature, and the influence of his family. He found joy and peace in a variety of activities as a child in East Palo Alto, California, which finally prepared him for his football career.

Adams showed a great degree of natural athleticism even as a young child. He stood out among his friends thanks to his agility, quickness, and coordination. In each sport he tried, his physical prowess made him stand out.

Early Sports Exposure: Adams's family was a major factor in his early exposure to sports. His father, Douglas Adams Sr., was interested in coaching young football teams, and his older brother, Fred, played football. The young Davante had his first taste of the sporting world thanks to this family link.

Davante Adams

Sports Participation: Before focusing on football, Adams played a variety of sports, including basketball and track & field. He was able to build a solid athletic foundation and a diversified skill set because of these encounters. He frequently achieved greatness in these sports, displaying his adaptability and competitive spirit.

Competitive Spirit: Adams' intrinsic competitive spirit served as a unifying theme throughout his early years. He was always looking to win and get better, whether he was playing pick-up games with friends or participating in organized sports. His commitment to improving his abilities and pushing himself to the limit was motivated by his competitive mindset.

Finding a Passion: Although Adams experimented with other sports, football ultimately won his heart. Football's unique blend of toughness, strategy, and teamwork struck a deep chord with him. His future ascent to success would be propelled by this enduring love of the game.

Davante Adams

Early Lessons: Adams learned priceless life lessons from playing sports at a young age. He gained knowledge of self-control, cooperation, the value of practice, and the highs and lows of competition. These teachings would be crucial in determining how he would play football and live his life off the field.

The basis for Davante Adams' eventual football success was his early interest in sports. He became a well-rounded athlete as a result of his exposure to a range of sports, competitive attitude, and family influences. The lessons he picked up during these formative years would play a crucial role in his path as he worked toward his goal of playing professional football.

CHAPTER 3: HIGH SCHOOL YEARS

The years that Davante Adams spent in high school were an important time in his life because they symbolized his transformation from a talented young athlete to a standout football player with a promising future. His love for the activity grew, his abilities improved, and he started to be recognized for his extraordinary gift during this period.

Adams went to Palo Alto High School, where he got the chance to demonstrate his athletic talents on a more official stage. He was given the framework and instruction he needed by the school's football program to hone his abilities and succeed.

Football Rising Star: Adams' talent was obvious to his coaches and teammates even in high school. He soon rose to prominence on the football field as a result of his quickness, agility, and capacity for game-changing plays. He stood out from his friends thanks to his inherent athleticism.

Position Flexibility: Adams' adaptability on the field was one of the main elements of his success. He showed that he could play both wide receiver and defensive back. His adaptability and willingness to participate in numerous positions to help the team out were demonstrated by his versatility.

Building Chemistry: Adams had the chance to establish crucial bonds and chemistry with his teammates throughout his time in high school. As he advanced to higher levels of competition, making connections with quarterbacks and other players would become a critical ability.

Acclaim and Awards: As his reputation increased, Adams started to get acclaim and awards for his on-field accomplishments. He was a force to be reckoned with thanks to his extraordinary speed, agility, and catching skills. His reputation as a standout athlete was further cemented by awards like All-League recognition.

College Recruitment: College recruiters took note of Adams' strong high school accomplishments. His exceptional receiving abilities and all-around athleticism caught the attention of college football coaches across the nation. This focus paved the way for his football career's subsequent chapter.

Adams' high school years gave him a solid foundation of skills, teamwork, and competitive spirit that would serve him well in the future. These traits would serve him well as he moved from youth football to college football and finally professional football.

In conclusion, Davante Adams' quick ascent to the position of top football player defined his high school years. The foundation for his future success was formed during his time at Palo Alto High School, which helped him develop his passion for the sport, hone his abilities, and put him on the route to being a well-known figure in the football community.

3.1: High school football experience

In a crucial period of his life, Davante Adams played football for Palo Alto High School, where he developed his abilities, reaffirmed his love for the game, and started to establish himself as a star performer.

Early Impact: Adams had a significant impact on the football field as soon as he joined the high school squad. His innate athleticism, quickness, and capacity for making plays attracted the attention of both coaches and players. Despite his diminutive size, he stands out for his tenacity and work ethic.

Position Change: Adams showed his versatility during his high school career by competing as both a wide receiver and a defensive back. His ability to adapt and willingness to help out wherever his team needed him most demonstrated his football IQ. It also demonstrated his aptitude for picking up new skills and excelling in all facets of the game.

Adams continued to hone his receiving abilities under the direction of his high school coaches. He practiced running routes, perfecting his catching technique, and learning the subtleties of the game. The basis for the refined player he would become was set by these efforts.

Team dynamics: Adams was able to form meaningful relationships with his teammates during his time in high school. The connection he developed with his teammates helped the squad to be cohesive and successful on the field because football is a team sport.

Achievements and Recognition: As his abilities grew, Adams received praise for his performances. His prominence as one of the league's best players was confirmed by awards including All-League recognition. These accolades not only increased his self-confidence but also caught the eye of college recruiters.

Davante Adams

College prospects: College football programs expressed interest in Adams as a result of his strong high school exploits. His transition to the collegiate level was facilitated by his adaptability, athleticism, and success on the field, which made him a desirable prospect for college recruiters.

Adams' involvement in high school football had a lasting influence on his life and profession. His subsequent success in college and the NFL was made possible by the lessons he learned about cooperation, self-control, and determination. The experiences and growth he went through during this time helped to mold his transformation from a brilliant high school football player to a professional football superstar.

In essence, Davante Adams' time playing football in high school was a significant turning point in his life. He improved his abilities, deepened his love for the game, and started to make a name for himself on the football field during this time.

3.2: Notable achievements

1. Davante Adams's college football career at Fresno State was distinguished by extraordinary accomplishments. He set numerous marks for receptions, receiving yards, and touchdowns at the school and conference levels. He was named a unanimous All-American and a semifinalist for the prestigious Biletnikoff Award, which is given to the greatest college football receiver in the country, because of his outstanding accomplishments.

2. Numerous nominations to the NFL Pro Bowl since joining the league demonstrate Adams' standing as one of the best wide receivers in the league. He has routinely received praise from teammates, coaches, and fans for his reliable productivity, route-running abilities, and capacity for making contested catches.

3. Franchise Records: The franchise records that Davante Adams owns demonstrate the impact he has had on the Green Bay Packers. He established new marks for

receptions in a season and receiving touchdowns, cementing his place in team lore alongside illustrious Packers receivers.

4. Bond with Aaron Rodgers: Adams' success has been largely attributed to his chemistry and relationship with Packers quarterback Aaron Rodgers. They have worked together on the field to produce many memorable plays, making them one of the NFL's most formidable quarterback-receiver combinations.

3.3: Challenges

1. Making the transition to the NFL: For any athlete, making the transition from college football to the NFL is a huge hurdle. At the professional level, Adams had to make the modifications necessary to adapt to a faster and more difficult game. Despite this, he showed his flexibility and became an important player right on.

2. Injuries: Adams, like many athletes, has dealt with injury issues during his career. A player's rhythm might

be broken by an injury, which can affect their performance. Adams has overcome adversity and returned to the field stronger because of his tenacity and drive, though.

3. Defensive Focus: Opposing defenses frequently focus on Adams because he is a top-tier wide receiver. This entails contending with double coverage, aggressive matchups and calculated defensive tactics designed to lessen his influence. It takes a combination of teamwork and individual expertise to overcome these obstacles.

4. High Expectations: Achieving a high degree of achievement entails a unique set of demands and standards. Adams has had to balance the burden of upholding his reputation, continually putting forth extraordinary performances, and assisting in his team's success.

5. Team Performance: Because football is a team sport, a player's success frequently hinges on how well the team as a whole performs. The Packers' overall success has

Davante Adams

sometimes limited Adams' opportunities and prominence. The ability to adapt and have a team-first perspective is necessary to overcome difficulties connected to team dynamics.

The journey of Davante Adams is evidence of his capacity to overcome obstacles and thrive on significant accomplishments. He continues to serve as an example for fans and aspiring athletes thanks to his achievements in college, NFL records, and overcoming the obstacles that come with playing professional football.

CHAPTER 4: COLLEGE JOURNEY

The collegiate experience for Davante Adams was a crucial stage that demonstrated his great talent, honed his football abilities, and equipped him for the difficulties of the NFL. He made notable advancements during his time at Fresno State University, experienced personal growth, and built a solid basis for his professional career.

Adams decided to pursue his schooling and football career at Fresno State University after graduating from high school. Making this choice was a crucial step in achieving his goals of playing at the collegiate level and beyond.

Adams quickly established himself as a prominent member of the Fresno State football team. He showed off his inherent athleticism and playmaking skills during his rookie season, emerging as a standout receiver. He developed a close relationship with his quarterbacks and won the respect of his coaches.

The record-breaking sophomore season was when Adams made a name for himself on the national stage. Incredibly, he set records for the school and the league with 131 grabs, 1,719 receiving yards, and 24 touchdowns. These numbers not only demonstrated his talent but also cemented his standing as one of the best receivers in college football.

Consistent Excellence: Adams showed exceptional consistency throughout his college career. He continued to produce well, demonstrating his capacity to provide at the highest level week after week. He was a crucial part of his team's offense thanks to his deft route running, dexterous hands, and capacity for making contested catches.

Awards and Recognition: Adams's accomplishments on the field were well-received. He was named a unanimous

Davante Adams

All-American, which elevated him to the top echelon of collegiate football players. He qualified as a semifinalist for the Biletnikoff Award, which is given to the top receiver in the country, because of his efforts.

Adams's journey through college was typical of the personal growth that students experienced throughout this time. His temperament and leadership skills were shaped by his experiences both on and off the field. He developed the ability to handle the rigors of both academics and athletics, further displaying his resolve and discipline.

Adams's college experience gave him access to a competitive atmosphere that helped him be ready for the rigors of the NFL. His accomplishments versus university defenses showed that he was prepared for the difficulties that professional football would present.

In conclusion, Davante Adams' time at Fresno State was distinguished by record-breaking successes, personal development, and the acquisition of talents that would lead to the height of his football prowess. The foundation for his move to the NFL was established throughout his time at the institution, which demonstrated his capacity to perform at the top level of collegiate football.

4.1: College selection process

The decision-making process for Davante Adams' college was a turning point in his football career because it dictated the route he would follow to pursue his goals of playing at the collegiate level and beyond. His choice of Fresno State University was eventually influenced by several things.

Recruitment: College recruiters were aware of Adams' extraordinary abilities and potential as a result of his high school football accomplishments. He was a sought-after recruit for collegiate programs because of his adaptability, quickness, and capacity to make plays on both offense and defense.

Davante Adams

Offers and Options: Adams was presented with several scholarship offers from several universities, each of which presented him with a special chance to advance both his academic and football careers. The choices he had to make were complicated by factors including the reputation of the program, the coaching staff, the amount of playing time, and the distance from home.

Finding a curriculum that complement Adams' playing style and talents was important in his decision-making process. He probably sought out a program that valued the passing game and could make the most of his wide receiver skills.

Coaching Team and Relationships: Adams's relationships with the coaching team during the hiring process, as well as their reputation and method, were key factors. He would have looked for coaches who had experience producing good receivers, believed in his ability, and could help him improve as a player.

Davante Adams

Opportunity for Early Influence: For recruiters, the chance to play and have an immediate influence on the field is frequently a key factor. Adams might have sought out a team where he could make an immediate contribution and display his potential as a young player.

Academic considerations: Student-athletes must balance their studies and athletics. Adams undoubtedly considered the academic programs and support provided by each college while deciding which one to attend, assuring he could succeed both on the field and in the classroom.

Family and Support System: The opinions and assistance of family members are frequently important in the decision-making process. His choice may have been influenced by factors like proximity to home and the possibility of his family attending games.

Long-Term Goals: Adams would have thought about how his college choice fit with his long-term objectives. He probably wanted to make the most of his chance for future football success, which can include opportunities at the professional level.

In the end, these elements came together to determine Davante Adams' college choice. His decision to attend Fresno State University demonstrated a program that recognized his potential, offered a positive playing environment, and gave him the chance to succeed in both athletics and academics. His great collegiate football career was launched by this choice, which also put him on the path to the NFL.

4.2: College football career and accomplishments

The Fresno State University football career of Davante Adams is evidence of his extraordinary talent, tenacity, and work ethic. He made an enduring impression on the Bulldogs during his time there and cemented his reputation as one of the most exciting wide receivers in college football history.

Davante Adams

Adams had a significant effect during his rookie year at Fresno State. Despite his inexperience at the collegiate level, the Bulldogs' quarterbacks were able to count on him to be a trustworthy target. The foundation for his future success was laid by his aptitude for making contested receptions and his knack for seeing open areas on the field.

Breakthrough as a second: Adams' second season was when he shocked the collegiate football world. He pulled together a season that broke records and made an enduring impression in the annals of history. With a spectacular 131 receptions, 1,719 receiving yards, and 24 touchdowns, Adams broke both school and conference records. His explosive performances in every game demonstrated his adaptability, speed, and capacity to change the course of a game.

Excellence Over Time: Adams's sophomore season wasn't just a one-off; he continued to perform at a high level throughout his collegiate career. Regardless of the opposition, he showed that he could constantly put up remarkable numbers. He was a terror for opposing teams thanks to his precise route running, strong hands, and capacity to add yards after the catch.

His amazing performances attracted national attention. Adams received significant acclaim, including unanimous All-American accolades. Additionally, he was included as a semifinalist for the Biletnikoff Award, which is presented to the top college football receiver in the nation. His standing among the top athletes in the sport was cemented by these honors.

Adams' influence on Fresno State went beyond numbers. He energized the Bulldogs' offense and raised spirit levels on the field. He wasn't just a game-changer; he was also a leader who motivated his team with his commitment and work ethic.

Adams's success at Fresno State helped him prepare for the difficulties of the NFL. Having faced collegiate defenses and performed well under duress, he gained the abilities and perspective necessary to be successful at the professional level.

In conclusion, Davante Adams' collegiate football career was distinguished by outstanding performances, record-breaking accomplishments, and an outstanding legacy. His tenure at Fresno State demonstrated his capacity for dominance on the field, enhancing his standing as one of the most talented receivers in the annals of collegiate football. His successes in college created the groundwork for his later success in the NFL and elsewhere.

CHAPTER 5: ENTERING THE NFL

An important turning point in Davante Adams' football career was when he joined the National Football League (NFL). After a stellar collegiate career, he started a new chapter full of chances, challenges, and the pursuit of his desire to play professional football at the highest level.

2014 NFL Draft: Following his redshirt sophomore year at Fresno State, Adams declared for the NFL Draft. He demonstrated his self-assurance and willingness to take on the demands of the NFL by forgoing his remaining college eligibility. He was chosen by the Green Bay Packers with the 53rd overall pick in the second round of the 2014 NFL Draft.

Professional Football shift: For Adams, joining the NFL was a huge shift. The professional league presented fresh difficulties that necessitated adaptation and development due to its speed, complexity, and level of competition. He needed to showcase himself in front of established stars and seasoned veterans on a bigger stage.

Green Bay Packers: Adams's NFL career started with the storied team that has a long history of producing talented receivers, the Green Bay Packers. Adams had a special chance to learn from one of the best in the game by joining a team coached by quarterback Aaron Rodgers.

Rookie Season and Early Impact: During his first NFL season, Adams rapidly established his legitimacy. He showed off his route-running skills, catching proficiency, and commitment to helping the Packers' offense. He was able to succeed in a variety of receiving positions thanks to his versatility, which won Rodgers and the coaching staff over to him.

Growth and Development: Adams underwent growth and development over his first few seasons in the NFL. He kept honing his techniques, adjusting to the quirks of professional football, and developing a rapport with his quarterback. He made steady progress because he was determined to get better and was prepared to put in the effort.

Breakout Years: Adams started to establish himself as a top wide receiver as he gained experience and became more used to the Packers' offense. He put up excellent numbers in terms of receptions, yards, and touchdowns during his breakout seasons. He consistently produced clutch plays and had a big impact when it mattered.

Dynamic partnership with Aaron Rodgers: Adams' relationship with quarterback Aaron Rodgers has been one of the highlights of his NFL career. They make a powerful team on the field thanks to their compatibility, timing, and confidence in one another's skills. This alliance has produced several noteworthy plays and plays that changed the course of games.

Records and Pro Bowl choices: Adams's superior performance on the field garnered him choices to the Pro

Bowl and catapulted him to the top echelon of NFL wide receivers. He further cemented his legacy with the Packers by shattering single-season and receiving touchdown records for the organization.

Years of laborious work, devotion, and persistence came to a head with Davante Adams's admission into the NFL. His tremendous talent and unrelenting dedication to the sport of football are evidenced by his capacity to adapt, learn, and excel in the professional football environment.

5.1: NFL Draft and rookie season

NFL Draft:

The 2014 NFL Draft served as the starting point of Davante Adams' NFL career. He had a stellar undergraduate career at Fresno State before declaring for the draft, demonstrating his capacity for professional competition. In the draft, teams eager to improve their receiving group were drawn to Adams's strong college résumé and explosive playmaking skills.

Davante Adams

Adams was chosen by the Green Bay Packers with the 53rd overall pick in the second round. His selection by a renowned team with a track record of developing elite receivers was evidence of both his potential and the high expectations that were placed on him.

The Green Bay Packers, rookie season:
Adams made his league debut with the Green Bay Packers during his rookie year. He encountered a higher standard of competitiveness, complexity, and expectations when he entered the professional arena. Here are some noteworthy events from his first year:

Learning Curve:
Adams entered the NFL with a solid talent set, but it took him some time to become used to the speed and complexities of professional football. He had to adjust to the defensive plans and tactics used by NFL teams, which necessitated knowing how to change his route, cover his body, and anticipate quarterback reads.

Contributions to the Offense:

Davante Adams

Adams, a rookie, made an immediate impact on the Packers' offense. He was a valuable target for quarterback Aaron Rodgers because of his steady hands, nimble route running, and capacity for gaining separation. He significantly increased his playing time and was an essential element of the receiving rotation for the club.

Trust and Chemistry:

Adams and Rodgers' relationship chemistry was one of the season's major features as a rookie. A young receiver must gain the confidence of a top quarterback. Adams was able to build a relationship with Rodgers that made it possible for him to be targeted in crucial circumstances and develop into a dependable option in the passing game.

Big Moments:

During his rookie season, Adams had several standout moments that demonstrated his promise. He demonstrated a talent for converting on important third-down plays by making clutch catches. These instances demonstrated his capacity to deliver when under pressure and support the Packers' offensive success.

Growth and Development:

Throughout his first season, Adams' development was clear. He grew from his mistakes, adapted to the demands of the NFL, and kept developing his knowledge of the game. As he adjusted to the job environment, his perseverance and work ethic were evident.

The groundwork for Davante Adams' future success in the NFL was laid during his rookie season. It gave him priceless experience, enabled him to establish himself as a key member of the Packers' offense, and prepared him for his future rise to the top of the league as a wide receiver.

5.2: Transition to professional football

When Davante Adams made the switch to professional football, it was a big turning point in his career and required adjustment to new pressures, circumstances, and standards. His transition from the NCAA to the NFL required him to make changes to his approach, thinking, and different areas of his game.

Speed and Complexity:

The speed and complexity of an NFL game required one of Adams' most urgent changes. The quick tempo of the game, the athleticism of the opposition, and the complex defensive tactics presented fresh difficulties. Adams had to think more quickly, decide more quickly, and change his course immediately.

Physicality and Competition:

When compared to college football, the NFL is more physically demanding. Adams had to deal with stronger, more skilled defenders who were skilled at sabotaging routes and disputing catches. His adjustment required him to hone his technique, efficiently use his body to gain separation and build the strength to compete for position with defensive backs of the caliber of an NFL.

Learning Curve and Playbook:

Understanding an NFL playbook is a difficult task. Adams had to become familiar with the language used in the Packers' offensive scheme as well as the intricate details of route modifications based on defensive coverages. Because of the steep learning curve, he needed to be committed, watch film, and practice often to be on the same page as his quarterback and coaches.

Physical and Mental Conditioning:

Compared to the college schedule, the NFL season is longer and more demanding. Adams had to adjust to the demands of a longer season, including the strain on his body from traveling, workouts, and games. His daily activities now included managing recovery and keeping himself in top physical condition. He also needed to strengthen his mental fortitude to deal with the highs and lows of playing professional football.

Davante Adams

Building Chemistry:

Adams' move required him to get along with Aaron Rodgers, his quarterback. Their connection depended heavily on building trust, figuring out time, and knowing where to be on the field in certain circumstances. It took time, effort, and great communication to establish this rapport.

Adams entered a world of increasing media scrutiny and public attention when he became a professional athlete. Adams had to manage interviews, public appearances, and the expectations of fans and the media while concentrating on his on-field performance because NFL players are subject to a considerably brighter spotlight.

Progress Over Time:

Adams' transformation was not just about short-term success, but also about progress over time. He needs to consistently work on his talents, be receptive to coach criticism, and be able to shift with the game. He would continue to hone his route running, catch techniques, and

Davante Adams

awareness of defensive coverages as he advanced in the NFL.

In conclusion, Davante Adams had to overcome difficulties relating to the physicality, speed, and intricacy of the playbook as he adjusted to professional football. It was a credit to his commitment, work ethic, and resolve to excel at the highest level of the sport that he was able to adapt, learn, and mature within the challenging atmosphere of the NFL.

Davante Adams

CHAPTER 6: OVERCOMING CHALLENGES

Davante Adams' capacity to overcome obstacles has been a defining quality of his route to success in football and life. He has faced challenges throughout his career that have put his resiliency, tenacity, and character to the test. Here are some strategies he used to overcome obstacles:

Childhood Adversity:

Growing up in East Palo Alto, California, Adams encountered difficulties as a result of the socioeconomic difficulties in his neighborhood. He refused to allow these circumstances, nonetheless, to define who he was. Instead, he utilized his challenging background as inspiration to play football and work for a brighter future.

Davante Adams

NFL transition Complexity:

There was a significant learning curve when moving from college football to the NFL. Adams had to become used to the increased speed, intricate defensive set-ups, and physicality of professional football. He overcame this obstacle by persistent study, practice, and a willingness to pick up tips from more knowledgeable peers.

Setbacks and Injuries:

An athlete's journey will inevitably include setbacks. At numerous periods in his career, Adams experienced setbacks brought on by injuries. He did, however, exhibit extraordinary resilience by rigorously recovering, keeping a positive outlook, and coming back to the field even more powerful than before.

Adams became a target for opposing defenders as his notoriety developed, drawing defensive attention and double coverage. He frequently dealt with double coverage and tactics intended to lessen his impact. To continue contributing effectively to his squad, he needed to adjust to new routes and means of establishing separation in addition to his skills.

Football is a team sport where individual achievement is frequently correlated with team success. The Green Bay Packers occasionally encountered difficulties as a team, which affected Adams's opportunities and statistics. Despite this, he remained committed to his job and made an effort to have a positive influence despite the situation.

Pressure and High Expectations:
Pressure and high expectations are a part of success. Adams has to deal with the stress of being a top receiver and putting forth reliable performances. He overcame this difficulty by remaining committed to his method, having faith in his planning, and allowing his performance on the field to speak for itself.

Building Relationships with Quarterbacks:
Adams's ability to connect with quarterbacks, notably Aaron Rodgers, is crucial to his success. It took time and

constant effort to get to know each other's timing, preferences, and habits to develop this chemistry. It took trust, repetition, and open communication to overcome this obstacle.

Beyond football, Adams has struggled with issues relating to his desire to improve personally and have a positive influence off the field. He has addressed social issues, pushed for constructive change, and given back to his neighborhood by using his position. It takes intention, empathy, and the capacity to effectively manage different roles to balance these obligations.

Davante Adams' journey essentially serves as a monument to his fortitude, adaptability, and resolve to overcome obstacles. His character as an athlete and as a person is demonstrated by his capacity to meet challenges head-on, learn from failures, and come out stronger. His narrative acts as motivation for people dealing with their difficulties by serving as a reminder that, with the correct attitude and work, adversities may be transformed into stepping stones toward achievement.

6.1: Injuries and setbacks

Davante Adams's football career has been distinguished by his capacity to recover from setbacks and injuries, exhibiting resiliency, perseverance, and a great work ethic. He has had numerous difficulties throughout his career, including injuries, which have pushed him to the limit and molded his character.

College ankle issue: While attending Fresno State, Adams suffered an ankle ailment that forced him to miss a few games. This setback might have derailed his progress, but his commitment to recovery and enthusiasm to get back on the field enabled him to overcome the injury and carry on contributing to his team.

2015 Ankle Injury: During his second NFL season with the Green Bay Packers, Adams suffered an ankle injury. Despite the loss, he hard worked to bounce back, displaying his commitment to helping his team succeed. He was able to get back on the pitch and keep improving as a vital player thanks to his dedication to his recovery and mental fortitude.

Concussion in 2015:

Adams also suffered a concussion in 2015. Concussions are severe injuries that call for meticulous treatment procedures. Adams and the Packers' medical staff put Adams' health first and made sure he took the right precautions to return to the field safely. His perseverance and dedication to the healing process paid off as he got back to his old self.

Adams suffered a toe injury in the 2019 season, which had an impact on his effectiveness. This was a serious difficulty because it affected his ability to cut and accelerate. Adams showed his willpower by playing through the discomfort, receiving the right medical attention, and controlling his workload.

Learning and resilience:

In each situation, Adams' response to injuries was an example of his resilience. He refused to let failures define him. Instead, he saw them as chances to grow, change, and become better. He was able to keep a positive attitude throughout difficult circumstances because of his mentality of concentrating on the variables he could control, such as his recovery, conditioning, and mental preparation.

Changing Up His Game:

Athletes may alter and improve their game as a result of injuries. Adams modified his routes and methods after suffering a toe injury to account for any physical restrictions. His capacity to adapt his strategy demonstrated both his football IQ and his commitment to finding ways to contribute in the face of difficulty.

Inspiration for Others:

Adams's perseverance in the face of setbacks serves as an example for both spectators and other athletes. His experience serves as a reminder of the value of persistence, patience, and a solid support network in the face of obstacles. Additionally, it supports the idea that failures are transient and can be used as a springboard for bigger successes.

In conclusion, Davante Adams's resilience in the face of adversity shows his everlasting resolve and mental toughness. His ability to persevere in the face of difficulties has been crucial to his climb to become one of the top wide receivers in the NFL, and his tale may serve as motivation for anybody trying to overcome problems and accomplish their objectives.

6.2: Personal growth

The development of Davante Adams as a person has been entwined with his football career, both on and off the field. He has demonstrated tremendous maturity, leadership, and a dedication to ongoing progress via his experiences, difficulties, and accomplishments.

Adams' background in East Palo Alto, a difficult environment, molded his character from a young age. Maturity through Adversity. He overcame socioeconomic hardship and learned to deal with the challenges of his environment. These encounters cultivated wisdom, fortitude, and an unwavering will to use football to improve the world.

Academic and athletic balancing:
Throughout his studies, Adams learned the value of maintaining a healthy balance between the two. Discipline and time management are required due to the obligations of being a student-athlete. He learned important life lessons from this balance, which he then used in his professional career.

Leadership both on and off the field:
Adams developed into a leadership figure as he advanced in football. He served as an inspiration to his colleagues, fans, and up-and-coming players thanks to his work ethic, passion, and capacity to lead by example. Along with his performance, he also showed leadership by improving team dynamics and the neighborhood.

Community Engagement:

Adams's involvement in philanthropic work showed that his personal development went beyond the playing field. As an NFL player, he was aware of his platform and made use of it to give back to the community. His dedication to having a significant impact was shown via his support for disadvantaged youngsters, advocacy for good change, and involvement in causes.

Managing Pressure and Expectations:

Success entails greater pressure and expectations. Adams had to live up to his reputation as a top receiver, which put pressure on him. His ability to bear the pressure to perform well speaks to his mental fortitude and personal development. He acquired the ability to perform well under pressure.

Accepting Change and Adaptation:

Adams showed flexibility as the NFL landscape changed. He had to modify his strategies and tactics due to changes in the coaching staff, team dynamics, and opponents. His capacity for adaptation shows that he is flexible and driven to succeed in a fast-paced atmosphere.

Family and Fatherhood:
For Adams, having a family and becoming a father constituted an important stage in his personal development. He learned new levels of maturity, responsibility, and priority from the responsibilities of parenting. His path as a parent demonstrates his dedication to continuing his personal growth beyond his football career.

Continuous Improvement Mindset:
Adams kept a mindset of continuous improvement throughout his trip. He aimed to hone his abilities, increase his depth of understanding of the game, and make a variety of contributions to his club. His dedication to pushing his limits and realizing his potential is highlighted by this growth-oriented strategy.

In conclusion, Davante Adams's growth journey is a tale of perseverance, leadership, flexibility, and a dedication to making a positive difference in his community and the globe. He used his time playing football as a platform for personal growth, and he made the most of those opportunities to become not only a world-class player but also an inspirational role model who emphasizes the importance of change and evolution.

6.3: Professional growth

The progress of Davante Adams as a professional is a reflection of his hard work, devotion, and desire to become the best wide receiver in the NFL. He has continually shown the traits that have helped him rise to the top of the game during his time in the league.

Improved Football Skills: Adams's continued improvement in his football abilities is a sign of his professional development. He has put a lot of effort into improving his catching technique, awareness of defensive coverages, and route running. His dedication to learning the specifics of his position has helped him constantly create separation and make crucial plays.

Davante Adams

Chemistry with Quarterbacks:

A wide receiver's success depends on his or her ability to develop a rapport with the quarterback. Adams has developed remarkably in this area. He has a strong rapport with Aaron Rodgers and the other quarterbacks he has played with because of his aptitude for recognizing quarterback tendencies, adapting to various throwing motions, and foreseeing throws.

Route Variety:

Adams has broadened his route repertoire since becoming a professional. From short, rapid routes to deep vertical routes, he has mastered the ability to excel in a variety of routes. His adaptability gives him a threat at all positions on the field, and his variety of routes confuses opponents.

Yards After Catch (YAC):

Adams's ability to move the ball after the catch has improved. After gaining possession of the ball, he has increased his agility, elusiveness, and decision-making, converting little gains into large yardage. He becomes a more potent playmaker thanks to his YAC ability, which gives his game an added dimension.

Recognizing Defensive Schemes:
Professional development entails improving one's capacity for seeing and responding to defensive strategies. Adams's football IQ has increased over the years, allowing him to analyze coverages, identify weak places in zone defenses, and take advantage of defensive flaws. He can make decisions more quickly on the field because of this recognition.

Performance & Consistency:
Adams' consistency has been a defining characteristic of his professional development. He has acquired the mental toughness to consistently perform at a high level. His capacity to produce memorable performances, regardless of the opposition or the situation, demonstrates his development as a dependable playmaker.

Davante Adams

Leadership and mentoring:

As his career has developed, Adams has accepted a leadership position on the squad. He adds to the culture of the squad as a whole, mentors younger players, and sets an example with his work ethic. His development as a leader is a reflection of his growing awareness of the wider influence he can have on the team.

Adapting to defenders:

As Adams's reputation grew, he began to attract more defenders' attention. His development entails adjusting to double coverage, tactical game plans, and defensive changes intended to contain him. His capacity for problem-solving and football IQ are evident from his ability to adjust to these difficulties.

In conclusion, Davante Adams's development as a professional is the result of his commitment, skill improvement, adaptability, and leadership. His rise from a promising rookie to one of the top receivers in the NFL is a testament to his never-ending development, mental

Davante Adams

toughness, and relentless dedication to realizing his full potential on the football field.

CHAPTER 7: RISE TO PROMINENCE

Davante Adams' ascent to fame is a fantastic story that highlights his tenacity, talent, and relentless dedication to becoming one of the top wide receivers in the NFL. Adams' rise has been defined by notable accomplishments and persistent pursuit of perfection from his early years to his current stature as a household celebrity.

College Breakout:
Adams' rise to fame began while he was a student at Fresno State University. A breakthrough moment during his second season propelled him into the national spotlight. Adams' outstanding performance earned him a spot on the consensus All-American team and qualified him for the prestigious Biletnikoff Award semifinals. He

set records for receptions, receiving yards, and touchdowns.

NFL Draft pick:

The Green Bay Packers' pick of him in the second round of the 2014 NFL Draft was a pivotal moment in his ascent to notoriety. The Packers were aware of his ability and the contribution he could make to their offense.

Early Years in the NFL:

Adams showed continuous improvement and progress during his early years in the NFL. He put in a lot of effort to hone his abilities, develop a rapport with quarterback Aaron Rodgers, and secure his position among the Packers' receiving group. He became more trustworthy as a target and saw his stats rise with each new season.

Breakout Seasons:

With a string of great seasons, Adams' journey to notoriety took off. His receptions, receiving yards, and touchdown totals were consistently spectacular. His efforts attracted the attention of spectators, pundits, and rivals alike, establishing him as one of the best receivers in the league.

Achievements That Broke Marks:
Adams joined the Hall of Fame of Packers receivers by breaking the franchise marks for receptions in a season and touchdown receptions. His propensity for scoring touchdowns and making big catches in critical situations contributed to his rise to prominence.

Chemistry with Aaron Rodgers:
Adams's success has been largely attributed to his compatibility with Aaron Rodgers. Their chemistry together on the pitch is evidence of their shared trust, expertise in the sport, and capacity to carry out precise maneuvers. There have been innumerable highlight-reel moments as a result of this cooperation.

His performance on the field earned him repeated Pro Bowl honors as well as praise from colleagues, coaches, and fans. With his accomplishments, Adams' name came to be associated with the best receiver play in the league.

Leadership and Consistency:

Adams's leadership abilities and steady output helped to further establish his notoriety. Along with his exceptional individual performance, he also set an excellent example for younger players, helped the team win, and mentored them.

Community Impact:

In addition to his accomplishments on the field, Adams was well-known for his influence off it. He promoted social change, participated in humanitarian activities, and helped his neighborhood by using his platform.

In conclusion, Davante Adams' ascent to fame is a story of adversity, tenacity, and ongoing development. His progression from a college breakout star to an NFL great demonstrates his capacity to overcome obstacles, seize opportunities, and consistently deliver at the very top of his game. His name has come to represent receiver excellence, and young athletes who aspire to compete at the highest levels of their sports can find motivation in his narrative.

7.1: Breakout seasons

The NFL seasons that marked Davante Adams's career turning point showed him developing into one of the top wide receivers in the game. His development throughout these seasons from a young, promising athlete to a powerful force on the field left a long-lasting impression on the Green Bay Packers offense and the league at large.

2016 Breakout Season:

Adams's first notable breakthrough came during the 2016 NFL season. He became a dependable target for quarterback Aaron Rodgers and was crucial to the Packers' offensive success. He and Rodgers' connection started to click, and as a result, he recorded career highs in receptions (75), receiving yards (997), and touchdowns (12).

2018 Breakout Season:

Adams' breakthrough in 2018 was even more impressive. He demonstrated his capacity to win games and make crucial plays. He displayed his adaptability, route-running skills, and aptitude for scoring touchdowns with 111 receptions, 1,386 receiving yards, and 13 scores. His place as one of the top receivers in the NFL was firmly established by this breakout season.

Adams' dominance carried over into the 2019 season after his breakthrough year in 2018. Despite playing in only 12 games due to injuries, he put up remarkable stats with 83 receptions, 997 receiving yards, and 5 touchdowns despite defensive strategies intended to restrict his effect. His performance demonstrated his capacity for overcoming obstacles and continued to be a key component of the Packers' attack.

Record-Breaking Season in 2020:

Adams had a record-breaking season in 2020. He set new franchise highs with 1,374 receiving yards, 115 receptions, and an incredible 18 touchdowns. He and Rodgers had a new level of synergy, and he regularly came up with big plays when they were needed. In the red zone, where he was practically unstoppable with his route-running and hands, his impact was most noticeable.

Adams received well-deserved credit for his standout seasons by being named to the All-Pro and Pro Bowl teams. He earned All-Pro recognition, demonstrating that people thought he was among the best players in the game at his position. His reputation as a top wide receiver was further enhanced by his multiple nominations to the Pro Bowl.

Clutch Performances:
Adams's breakthrough seasons were marked by his capacity to perform under pressure. He frequently scored touchdowns when his team most needed them and made important catches on third downs and long drives. He gained the admiration of teammates and supporters alike for his dependability under pressure.

Davante Adams

Route Running and Separation:

One of Adams' breakout seasons' defining characteristics was his honed route running and capacity for creating separation. A threat on short, moderate, and deep routes, he displayed a broad route tree. He was able to constantly find openings thanks to his deft footwork, accuracy, and comprehension of defensive coverages.

Legacy of Excellence:

The Green Bay Packers and the NFL's histories will forever bear witness to Adams's standout seasons. His accomplishments have propelled him to the top tier of receivers, and his contributions on the field have created an outstanding legacy that will be remembered for years to come.

In conclusion, Davante Adams's breakthrough seasons were critical turning points that enabled him to advance to the position of most dominant wide receiver in the NFL. His unquestionable influence on the game of football was demonstrated by his ability to routinely produce outstanding performances, create game-changing plays, and set records.

7.2: Standout performances

Numerous outstanding performances during Davante Adams' career have cemented his place among the top wide receivers in the NFL. These performances highlight his dominance on the field, ability to make pivotal plays, and ability to carry his team to victory in the most critical situations.

Week 3, 2016:

Adams had a standout effort against the Detroit Lions in Week 3 that demonstrated his propensity for huge plays. He grabbed two touchdown passes from Aaron Rodgers, the quarterback, including one that he made with one hand despite being closely covered. His performance suggested that he might develop into one of the league's elite receivers.

2017 Playoffs, Divisional Round: In the Packers' triumph over the Dallas Cowboys in the 2017 Playoffs Divisional Round, Adams was a key contributor. Eight passes were caught by him for 125 yards and a significant touchdown. His club advanced in the playoffs because of his ability to make contested catches and earn yards after the catch.

Week 1 of 2018:

Adams' performance against the Chicago Bears in the season opener was illustrative of his capacity to excel under pressure. He grabbed a 12-yard touchdown pass and a two-point conversion in the fourth quarter despite the Packers trailing by 17 points. His performances helped the Packers win a dramatic comeback victory after forcing overtime.

Week 4, 2019:

Adams put on a commanding effort against the Philadelphia Eagles in Week 4 that highlighted his bond with quarterback Aaron Rodgers. He hauled in 10 passes for 180 yards and three touchdowns, one of which was an incredible game-winning catch in the fourth quarter. He made excellent use of his skills to locate open areas and make challenged receptions.

Week 10, 2020:

Adams put on a brilliant performance against the Jacksonville Jaguars in Week 10 of the 2020 campaign, showcasing his route-running accuracy and catch flexibility. Twelve receptions for 196 yards and two touchdowns were totaled by him. The Packers' victory was made possible by his persistent ability to get away from defenders and earn yards after the catch.

The Packers' performance against the Los Angeles Rams in the NFC Divisional Round of the 2020 Playoffs was crucial to their triumph. Nine passes were grabbed by him for 66 yards and an important touchdown. In a crucial playoff game, his capacity to advance the ball and make contested receptions displayed his dependability under duress.

Records and Milestones:

Davante Adams

Many of Adams' outstanding performances have set records and achieved significant milestones. He currently holds the franchise record for both receiving touchdowns and receptions in a season. He has earned a reputation as a record-setter thanks to his ability to successfully cross the goal line and have an impact on the game.

Consistency in Big Moments:
Adams stands out for his ability to consistently turn in outstanding performances when the stakes are high. Adams's ability to constantly perform above expectations defines his legacy as a standout player, whether it is by making the game-winning grab, converting on third downs, or scoring touchdowns in critical moments.

In conclusion, Davante Adams's remarkable accomplishments are a result of his extraordinary skill set, compatibility with quarterbacks, and capacity to perform well under pressure for his team. He has had an irreplaceable impact on the sport with his clutch performances, records, and game-changing events that have solidified his position as one of the top wide receivers in the NFL.

7.3: Establishing himself as a top receiver

Due to his exceptional skill set, perseverance, and on-field performance, Davante Adams has become a top receiver in the NFL. From his early years to his current position, Adams' path to becoming a great receiver has been marked by determination, growth, and the ability to consistently produce excellent performances.

Mastering the Trade:

Adams' ascent to notoriety as a top receiver began with his dedication to understanding the specifics of his position. He became better at running routes, receiving balls, and understanding defensive coverages. His success was enabled by his commitment to developing his talent.

Chemistry with Quarterbacks:

Davante Adams

Adams' ascent has been primarily credited to his aptitude for forging bonds with quarterbacks, particularly Aaron Rodgers. Thanks to his ability to swiftly modify his routes, quickly assess defenses, and effectively communicate with his quarterbacks, he has developed into a dependable and dynamic target in several situations.

Top receivers are known for making plays in crucial moments that can decide games. Adams' dependability in urgent situations has defined his career. He consistently delivers on important third downs, in the end zone, and during drives that decide games. He is notable due to his propensity to become a prime target when under pressure.

Route Running and Separation:
Adams' outstanding route-running skills were crucial to his rise to fame. Because of his precise cuts, fast changes of direction, and capacity to elude defenders, any CB would struggle to cover him. His aptitude for running

routes has had a significant impact on his consistent productivity.

One of Adams' strengths is his ability to gain a lot of yardage after making the grab. He can turn fleeting receptions into significant gains thanks to his deception, athleticism, and vision. The offensive success of his squad as well as his numbers are both increased by this YAC skill.

Adams needed to produce consistently throughout a few seasons to establish himself as a top receiver. He accomplished this by regularly posting compelling statistics. His ability to rack up receiving yards and consistently high touchdown and grab totals have solidified his place among the league's top players.

Adams' performance has been praised by his teammates, coaches, supporters, and members of the media. Records broken, All-Pro honors, and Pro Bowl selections are all tangible evidence of his talent. He is among the best in his position, which speaks much about his impact on the game.

Getting Used to Defensive Focus: Defenses usually pay attention to leading receiver Adams. His ability to succeed despite double coverage and defensive strategies meant to reduce his influence speaks much about his adaptability and football IQ. He consistently finds a way to make an impact, even when defenders focus on stopping him.

Adams' standing as a top receiver extends beyond his on-field successes. To help younger players and improve the Packers' offense as a whole, he has accepted leadership and mentoring responsibilities within the team.

Davante Adams' growth as a top receiver has been characterized by his skill mastery, reliability in pivotal moments, consistency, and capacity for growth. He ranks among the best wide receivers in the NFL thanks to his efforts on the field, his successes, and his reputation as a top performer, forever altering the game of football.

Davante Adams

CHAPTER 8: PLAYING STYLE AND SKILLS

The playing style and abilities of Davante Adams make him one of the NFL's most exciting and productive wide receivers. Because of his special combination of abilities, he excels in many different areas of the game, making him a powerful force on the field.

Route Running Accuracy:
Adams' playing style is built around his precise route running. He excels at performing accurate cuts, selling fakes, and separating from defenders. Even when facing elite cornerbacks, his attention to detail in his routes enables him to regularly get open.

Release Technique:
His ability to get off the line of scrimmage quickly and effectively opens up his routes. Adams may start with a

Davante Adams

competitive advantage over opponents thanks to his swift first step and awareness of defensive leverage. He puts pressure on opposing cornerbacks to react swiftly with his release technique.

Adams excels at making contested receptions, showing off his powerful hands, timing, and body control. He is adept at high-pointing the ball, using his stature to block defenders, and keeping his composure while taking hits. He is a dependable target in close coverage and on jump balls because of this ability.

Adams's elusiveness and athleticism after the catch greatly contribute to his performance in the yards after catch (YAC) category. He can turn brief receptions into substantial gains thanks to his fast changes of direction, ability to break tackles, and ability to maneuver through traffic. His playing style gains a dynamic element from his YAC skill.

Adams is renowned for his accuracy when running routes, but he can also pose a threat on deep passes. He excels at vertical routes with his speed and tracking abilities, and he can connect on long throws thanks to his rapport with quarterbacks. This adaptability throws off defenses and widens the playing field for the offensive.

Adams's playing style excels in the red zone, where he has dominance. He is a popular target close to the goal line because of his rapid separation and knack for taking advantage of mismatches. He is a great choice in crucial scoring circumstances due to his adeptness at locating wide spaces and precise route running.

Throws:

Adams' ability to react to off-target throws is one of his strongest traits. Adams's body control and spatial awareness enable him to make challenging receptions in several circumstances, including back-shoulder passes, balls delivered high or low, or throws that demand him to modify his route mid-play.

Davante Adams

Synergy with Quarterbacks:

Adams's remarkable synergy with his quarterbacks, particularly Aaron Rodgers, amplifies his skills. They have produced a lot of big plays and touchdowns thanks to their knowledge of timing, anticipation, and improvisation. Adams can make big plays downfield and perform well in scramble situations thanks to this synergy.

Field awareness and versatility:

Adams's ability to line up in a variety of spots on the field demonstrates his versatility. He can take advantage of matchups and alter his route depending on the alignment of the defense thanks to his football IQ and field awareness. His adaptability enables him to have an impact wherever on the field and keeps opponents on their toes.

In conclusion, Davante Adams combines his ability to execute precise routes with contested catches, YAC skill, and deep-threat potential in his playing style. He is a versatile receiver with skills who can perform well in a variety of settings, and his rapport with quarterbacks increases the effect of his play. His abilities and playing style make him a dynamic and commanding presence on the field.

8.1: Analysis of his playing style

Analyzing Davante Adams's playing style requires a thorough investigation of his advantages, methods, and effects on the field. His prominence as one of the top wide receivers in the NFL is a result of his distinctive skill set and personal qualities.

Excellent Route Running:

Adams' playing style is characterized by his route running. He moves with outstanding fluidity, accuracy, and footwork. His success is largely down to his capacity to blast off the line, execute fast cuts, and create separation with subtle movements. He frequently gains distance from defenders thanks to his route running, which makes him a safe target for his quarterbacks.

Davante Adams

Release and footwork:

A key element of his playing style is his release off the line of scrimmage. Adams can evade press coverage and take on defenders at the line because of his quick release and fluid technique. His efficient release style establishes the tone for his routes and aids in his early-play advantage.

Adams' talent for making contested receptions demonstrates his great hands, body control, and timing. He is excellent at positioning his body to block defenders' access to the ball, and he makes strong catches in close coverage with his upper body. Due to this talent, he is a dependable target in high-stakes and danger zones.

Ability to Gain Yards After Catch (YAC):

Adams's playing style heavily depends on his capacity to gain yards after the catch. His dexterity, stability, and vision enable him to maneuver through traffic and gain extra yards. Short receptions become large gains thanks to his YAC talent, putting him in a position to break off big plays.

His adaptability is a crucial component of his playing style, as is his route tree. Adams is proficient on a variety of routes because of his wide-ranging route tree and ability to line up both inside and outside. He is skilled in every aspect of receiving, which keeps defenses on their toes, from short, fast routes to deep vertical patterns.

Adams's playing style excels in the red zone, as his blend of route running, contested catch prowess, and body control make him a go-to target. His rapid separation skills and spatial awareness help him be effective in the end zone and produce touchdowns.

Chemistry with Quarterbacks:
Adams' superb rapport with his quarterbacks, especially Aaron Rodgers, enhances his playing style. They can execute timing-based routes, back-shoulder throws, and improvised plays with amazing efficiency thanks to their

rapport. His total impact on the field is enhanced by this chemistry.

Adams' flexibility and football IQ are two of his less obvious but no less important qualities. He can modify his routes depending on coverage, take advantage of mismatches, and locate open spaces thanks to his football IQ and defense-reading skills. This versatility demonstrates his profound knowledge of the game.

Consistency in Tough Situations:
Adams' playing style is characterized by his dependability in tough circumstances. He performs best when the outcome of the game is in doubt, making critical catches while utilizing his route running, catch radius, and mental stability. His capacity to perform well under pressure solidifies his reputation as a trustworthy playmaker.

In conclusion, Davante Adams's game combines his skill at route running with his strength at contested catches, his YAC prowess, and his versatility. He is a dominant force on the field because of his compatibility with quarterbacks, adaptability, and capacity for excellence under pressure. His reputation as one of the top wide receivers in the NFL is largely owed to his special combination of abilities.

8.2: Key strengths

Davante Adams is one of the top wide receivers in the NFL thanks to a variety of important qualities. These qualities are essential to his playing style and have been crucial in making him a tyrannical force on the field.

Accurate Route Running:

Adams' ability to take accurate routes is one of his most notable abilities. Sharp cutbacks, deft fakes, and swift direction changes are all ways he excels at getting away from opponents. He frequently gets open and makes plays because of his superb route-running accuracy.

Davante Adams

Contested Catch Ability:

Adams excels at making contested receptions thanks to his powerful hands, body awareness, and timing. He performs best when he is fully covered by defenders because he can use his size and agility to make challenging catches. He is a dependable target in urgent circumstances thanks to his contested catch abilities.

His flexibility off the line of scrimmage is a significant strength. Adams can take advantage of defensive leverage and his quick footwork to establish a lead immediately after the play. His early separation in the play is aided by his release technique, providing his quarterbacks a chance to target him.

Yards After Catch (YAC) Prowess:

Adams stands out for his exceptional YAC skills. He can avoid tacklers and gain significant yardage after making a grab thanks to his quickness, balance, and vision. A dynamic element to his game is added by his elusiveness and capacity to turn brief receptions into substantial advantages.

Davante Adams

Route Tree's versatility:
Adams' adaptability is another major asset. He is skilled at running a variety of routes, including deep vertical patterns and short, rapid slants. His broad route tree makes him adaptable to various attacking strategies and keeps defenses off guard.

Body Control and Adjustments:
His ability to change passes mid-air demonstrates his body control. Adams's body control enables him to complete challenging receptions, whether it's following the ball over his shoulder, adapting to back-shoulder throws, or bending his body to make catches in confined places.

Adams's combination of qualities is what drives his supremacy in the red zone. He is a prime target close to the end zone because of his route running, contested catch ability, and spatial awareness. One important strength that significantly adds to his high touchdown productivity is his ability to be productive in confined situations.

Davante Adams

Timing and Chemistry:

His rapport with quarterbacks, especially Aaron Rodgers, is a key asset. They can execute plays properly because of their timing and awareness of one another's inclinations. Along with his quarterbacks, Adams's ability to read the defense boosts his overall effectiveness on the field.

Consistency and Reliability:

His reliable performance is one of his biggest assets. No matter the opponent or the situation, Adams continually puts out strong performances. He is a valuable player for his squad because of his dependability as a target for his quarterbacks and his capacity for consistency.

Adams's capacity to make significant plays in pressure situations is one of her defining strengths. He excels under duress, displaying his mental stability, route-running accuracy, and trusty hands. He is a go-to player in urgent situations because of his clutch playmaking.

In conclusion, Davante Adams's accurate route running, contested catch ability, YAC skill, adaptability, and overall dependability comprise his primary qualities. He is a dynamic and effective wide receiver with the ability to dominate defenses and continuously influences the game because he combines skills.

8.3: Contributions to the team and Sport

Davante Adams has made significant and far-reaching contributions to the Green Bay Packers as well as the game of football as a whole. His on-field prowess, leadership, and commitment to enhancing the game have made a lasting impression on both levels.

Efforts on behalf of the Green Bay Packers:

1. Offensive Anchor: The Packers' offense has been anchored by Adams. His dependable top-tier receiving performance has given the team's passing game stability and dependability.

Davante Adams

2. Go-To Target: Adams is a quarterbacks' go-to target because of his propensity to make big catches in crunch time, especially for Aaron Rodgers. His presence gives the offense a dependable means of making significant gains and moving the chains.

3. Dominance in the Red Zone: The Packers' efficiency in scoring has been greatly impacted by Adams' skill in the red zone. He has made many contested catches and found gaps, which has resulted in many scores and helped the team win.

4. Leadership and Mentorship: As an experienced player, Adams has acted as a mentor to younger players both on and off the field. His dedication, readiness, and upbeat demeanor served as role models for his coworkers and promoted an excellence-oriented environment.

5. Locker Room Presence: Adams's character and friendship with teammates have helped the team to gel and be cohesive. The Packers' entire dynamic is

improved by his pleasant interactions and capacity to connect with players in every position.

Sports contributions:

1. Redefining Receiver Play: The way receivers handle contested catches, separation methods, and route running has been inspired by Adams' playing style. For aspiring wide receivers, his footwork, agility, and physicality have become models.

2. Route-Running Emphasis: Adams' outstanding route-running abilities have brought attention to how crucial accuracy is in this area of the game. His expertise with route intricacies and capacity for separation have turned into a teaching and development focus.

3. Yards After Catch (YAC) Emphasis: Adams' capacity to gain big yardage after the catch highlights the significance of this element of offensive strategy. His accomplishments have inspired clubs to use short-passing plays that let receivers demonstrate their elusiveness.

Davante Adams

4. Wide Receiver-QB Chemistry: Adams's relationship with his quarterbacks demonstrates the importance of wide receivers and their quarterbacks building chemistry. He has established a benchmark for the cooperation between pass catchers and passers thanks to his ability to anticipate throws and adapt to various quarterbacks.

5. Motivation for Young Athletes: Adams' transformation from an under-recruited high school player to an NFL superstar serves as motivation for young athletes. His experience serves as proof that perseverance, hard effort, and determination may result in extraordinary achievement.

6. Social Justice Advocacy: Adams's use of his position to promote social justice and constructive change exemplifies the part that athletes may play in resolving significant societal problems. His activism serves as an example of the wider influence sportsmen can have outside of their sport.

Davante Adams

In conclusion, Davante Adams has made contributions to the Green Bay Packers and the game of football that go above and beyond his numbers. He serves as an example for aspiring sportsmen and other professionals because to his impact on his team's performance, his impact on receiver play, and his dedication to making changes for the better. His legacy is one of excellence, leadership, and using one's position to advance society and the game.

CHAPTER 9: ACHIEVEMENTS AND RECORDS

Records and accomplishments during Davante Adams' illustrious career serve as a testament to his extraordinary talent and contribution to the game. His excellent play has earned him countless honors, landmarks, and franchise records that have cemented his reputation as one of the top wide receivers in the NFL.

Records held by the Green Bay Packers: Adams is the holder of several noteworthy franchise records, highlighting his significance in the organization's history. In terms of receptions, yards, and touchdowns in a single season of receiving, he holds the records. These accomplishments demonstrate his power in a variety of statistical subsets.

Davante Adams

Adams has frequently surpassed the coveted 1,000-yard receiving mark, which is a credit to his toughness and high standard of performance. His consistency in delivering highlights how important he is to the offense of the squad.

Adams has been chosen for many Pro Bowls as a result of his outstanding play, emphasizing his status as one of the greatest wide receivers in the league. His selection to the Pro Bowl shows how his fellow players value his talent and contribution to the game.

All-Pro Honors: Adams' All-Pro selections attest to his status as one of the top receivers in the NFL. These awards, which highlight his exceptional season-long performance, highlight his status as one of the best players in his position.

Adams has earned a reputation as a touchdown machine thanks to his consistent ability to find the end zone. His outstanding touchdown totals place him among the league leaders and highlight his talent for making pivotal plays.

Performances in clutch situations: Throughout his career, Adams has made significant catches at critical times, enhancing his reputation as a clutch player. He has produced memorable late-game heroics, game-winning catches, and crucial third-down conversions thanks to his ability to perform under duress.

Records set in a single game: Adams has led the Packers in receptions and receiving yards in a single game. His capacity to put on overpowering performances within the confines of a single game demonstrates his adaptability and ability to take charge when necessary.

His relationship with quarterback Aaron Rodgers has led to numerous milestones and accomplishments for both players. Numerous touchdown hookups have resulted from their collaboration, demonstrating their synergy and influence on the Packers' offense.

Impact on Team Success: During his stint with the Packers, Adams' contributions have significantly contributed to the team's overall success. His efforts have contributed to a winning culture by helping the team win divisions, make the playoffs, and go far in the postseason.

In conclusion, Davante Adams' accomplishments and statistics showcase his dependability, influence, and excellence as a wide receiver in the NFL. His All-Pro accolades, Pro Bowl selections, and club records highlight his importance to the sport and his squad. Adams's ability to produce consistently at a high level, leaving a permanent imprint on the game of football, solidifies his legacy.

9.1: Pro Bowl selections

The fact that Davante Adams was chosen for the Pro Bowl is evidence of his tremendous talent, dependable performance, and status as one of the top wide receivers in the NFL. Being chosen for the Pro Bowl is a big honor because it shows that Adams is one of the greatest at his position in the eyes of the public, coaches, and other athletes.

Adams was first chosen for the 2017 Pro Bowl following the 2016 NFL season. He recorded 75 receptions, 997 receiving yards, and 12 touchdowns, showcasing his development as a premier receiver. He received accolades from the league for his capacity to establish separation, make contested catches, and contribute to the offensive success of the Packers.

Adams was chosen for the 2018 Pro Bowl because of his outstanding 2017 campaign as a receiver. He recorded 74 receptions, 885 receiving yards, and 10 touchdowns despite dealing with ailments. He overcame obstacles and maintained a high level of performance, which demonstrated his tenacity and tenacity.

Adams was chosen for his third straight Pro Bowl in the 2018 season, continuing his impressive play. 111 receptions for 1,386 yards and 13 touchdowns despite missing four games due to injury. He showed off his exceptional grab range, route-running skills, and relationship with quarterback Aaron Rodgers.

Adams was chosen for the 2020 Pro Bowl as a result of his consistency and contribution to the Packers' offense in the 2018–19 campaign. He has 83 receptions for 997 yards and 5 touchdowns despite missing four games. His prowess in the face of defensive scrutiny underlined his importance to the team.

Adams was chosen for the 2021 Pro Bowl as a result of his outstanding performance in the 2020 season, which further cemented his status as one of the top wide receivers in the NFL. With 115 receptions, 1,374 receiving yards, and 18 touchdowns, he broke all previous marks for the team. His exceptional season served as a display of his adaptability, route-running accuracy, and rapport with his quarterbacks.

Adams was chosen for the 2022 Pro Bowl, which was his sixth selection overall. This honor was given to him following the 2021 campaign. He amassed 113 receptions for 1,429 yards and 10 touchdowns despite defensive strategies intended to lessen his effect. His reputation as a top receiver was cemented by his ability to consistently deliver at a high level.

In conclusion, Davante Adams's Pro Bowl choices are evidence of his talent, commitment, and influence on football. He is regarded as one of the league's top wide receivers thanks to his ability to constantly deliver at a high level, overcome obstacles, and help his team succeed. Each Pro Bowl selection he receives marks a turning point in his career and strengthens his standing in the NFL.

9.2: Team Records

Davante Adams has had a significant impact on the Green Bay Packers that extends beyond his accomplishments. He has permanently altered the team's record books. Numerous team records that illustrate his importance to the franchise are the consequence of his

Davante Adams

consistently exceptional play and outstanding
performances.

Adams currently maintains the team record for the most
receptions made in a single season. During the 2020
season, he broke the previous record with 115 receptions,
demonstrating his dependability and rapport with his
quarterbacks. His standing in Packers history was
cemented by his ability to regularly advance the chains
and make crucial catches.

Adams holds the single-season record for receiving
yards at wide receiver, which demonstrates his skill. He
broke the old franchise record with 1,374 receiving yards
in the same 2020 season. This incredible
accomplishment was made possible by his prowess on
deep routes and his ability to gain substantial yardage
after the catch.

Adams set a franchise record for touchdowns in a single
season in 2020 because of his incredible output. He set a
new Packers record with 18 receiving touchdowns,

scoring 18 of them. Numerous trips to the end zone resulted from his command of the red zone, accurate route running, and connection with his quarterbacks.

Adams has scored a touchdown on a receiving play in the most consecutive games (a team record), according to the statistics. His usefulness as a dependable scoring threat for the Packers' offense is highlighted by his ability to routinely find the end zone throughout a string of games.

Duo with the Most Receiving Touchdowns in a Season: Adams and quarterback Aaron Rodgers set a team record for the most touchdowns with the most receptions in a season. A record-breaking amount of touchdowns were scored throughout the 2020 season as a result of their remarkable synergy and ability to connect in the end zone.

Receptions by a Duo Together in a Season: Adams and Rodgers also established a team record for the total receptions by a duo together in a season. An incredible number of receptions were made possible in the 2020 season by their connection and Adams' ability to continually find openings.

Adams's ability to score from inside the 20 frequently resulted in a team record for the number of games in which he scored a receiving touchdown. He was able to compile this excellent record and add to the team's offensive success because of his dependability as a scoring threat.

Years with 10+ Receiving Touchdowns: Adams' repeated years with double-digit receiving touchdowns solidify his reputation as a prolific scorer. His importance on the Packers' offense is highlighted by his ability to consistently find the end zone over several seasons.

In conclusion, Davante Adams' influence on the Green Bay Packers is indelible in the team's history. He has become one of the most productive wide receivers in team history thanks to his single-season records, output of touchdowns, and consistency. These accomplishments serve as evidence of his talent, tenacity, and lasting influence with the Packers.

9.3: League records

While Davante Adams has left a significant mark on the Green Bay Packers record books, his accomplishments extend beyond the team level. He has also set and approached various league records that emphasize his impact on the broader NFL landscape.

Single-Game Receptions Record:
Adams came close to breaking the NFL record for the most receptions in a single game during the 2020 season. In a Week 7 matchup against the Houston Texans, he caught 13 passes, just one shy of tying the record for most receptions in a single game.

Consecutive Games with a Receiving Touchdown:
Adams's streak of consecutive games with a receiving touchdown, while setting a Packers record, also put him in the conversation for league history. His ability to

consistently find the end zone showcased his status as one of the NFL's premier scoring threats.

Consecutive Games with 5+ Receptions and 50+ Yards:

Adams's consistency in terms of receptions and yardage during a streak of games put him in elite company. He joined a short list of players in NFL history to record five or more receptions and 50 or more receiving yards in multiple consecutive games.

Seasons with 100+ Receptions and 10+ Touchdowns:

Adams's ability to achieve both 100+ receptions and 10+ touchdowns in a season places him among the league's top receivers. His combination of high-volume catches and red-zone scoring prowess is a rare and coveted trait.

Impact on Packers Franchise Records:

While not official NFL records, Adams's impact on the Packers' franchise records speaks to his league-wide influence. He has set team records for single-season receptions, single-season receiving yards, and single-season receiving touchdowns, reflecting his elite status within the league.

Recognition Among League's Elite:

Adams's consistent Pro Bowl selections, All-Pro honors, and inclusion in discussions about the best wide receivers in the NFL underscore his recognition as a top player at his position. While not recorded in the traditional sense, these accolades reflect his impact on the league's perception of his abilities.

In summary, while Davante Adams's league records might not rival some of the most historic NFL milestones, his accomplishments, consistency, and impact on the game place him among the top echelon of wide receivers. His influence on the Packers' record books and his recognition among the league's elite players highlight his legacy in the NFL.

CHAPTER 10: PERSONAL LIFE

Davante Adams' incredible football career is well-known, but his personal life also sheds light on the person behind the athlete. His childhood, family, interests, and principles help us comprehend who he is off the field on a more complete level.

Background information on the family:
Davante Adams was born in Redwood City, California, on December 24, 1992. He was raised in a loving, close-knit family. His parents were very important in his life since they encouraged his love of athletics and laid the groundwork for him to become a professional athlete.

Douglas Adams, Adams' father, had a significant impact on both his life and his growth as an athlete. He encouraged Davante's sporting endeavors and introduced him to several sports at a young age. Davante's early interest in athletics and his ambition to succeed were influenced by the close relationship between his father and son.

Academic pursuits:

Adams attended Palo Alto High School in California, where he excelled both academically and on the football field. His commitment to both studies and athletics demonstrated his self-control and well-rounded way of life.

Supportive Family Network:

Adams's family has remained a source of encouragement and support for him throughout his football career. He frequently discusses the value of his family's constant support and how they helped him mold his character both on and off the field.

Davante Adams

Community Involvement:
Adams's dedication to having a positive influence
extends to his involvement in the community. He
participates in initiatives and humanitarian work aimed
at enhancing the lives of those who are less fortunate.
His commitment to giving back is a reflection of his
principles and the impact he wants to have outside of
football.

Adams's personal life changed when he became a father,
and this led to his personal growth. His life outside of
football was given new meaning and depth with the birth
of his daughter, Davante Jr. Fatherhood has given him
new insight and rekindled his passion for both his
professional and personal goals.

Hobbies and hobbies:
Aside from sports, Adams has a wide range of hobbies.
He has exhibited an interest in music, and his love of
making and appreciating music gives him a platform for
self-expression. His well-rounded identity is influenced
by his diverse interests.

Relationship with Fans:

Adams's interactions with fans show how much he values their encouragement. He appreciates the value of his platform and frequently interacts with followers on social media and in local gatherings so they may get to know him better.

In conclusion, Davante Adams is lauded for his football accomplishments, but his personal life also shows that he is a kind, family-oriented guy who appreciates his roots, gives back to the community, and finds fulfillment in a variety of facets of life. His personal experience has complemented his athletic path and helped him develop into the well-rounded person he is today.

10.1: Family and relationships

Family and connections have a big impact on Davante Adams' life, both on and off the football field. His upbringing, relationships with his family, and interpersonal interactions provide clues about his personality, beliefs, and social network.

Davante Adams

Support from family:

Adams's family has been a pillar in his life and work. His close-knit family supported his sports endeavors from an early age when he was growing up. The foundation for his future success was laid by his parents' encouragement and his father's influence in getting him interested in sports.

Bond with his daughter, Davante Jr.: As a father, Adams's bond with his daughter has enriched his personal life. He frequently shows his daughter his love and attention, demonstrating his dedication to being an involved and loving dad. His life now has a new sense of meaning as a father.

Partner and Relationships:

Adams has maintained a somewhat discreet romantic life, including his marriage. He respects his privacy and keeps his sexual relationships somewhat of a secret. His dedication to his family, work, and community activity shows that he leads a balanced life.

Davante Adams

Relationships with Coworkers:
Within the Green Bay Packers organization, Adams's connections with his coworkers are crucial. His friendship with teammates enhances the chemistry and cohesiveness of the team. He mentors and leads by example, promoting a supportive team environment in his interactions with teammates.

Adams's relationships with his fans are a significant part of his public persona. He frequently interacts with his fan base on social media and at local events because he values their support. His interactions with the audience reveal how approachable he is and how appreciative he is of their support.

Community Engagement:
Adams' connections go beyond his immediate social circle to include his involvement in the community. Through charity endeavors and initiatives, he establishes connections with those in need while using his platform to make a difference. His dedication to giving back demonstrates his morals and sense of accountability.

Adams need to strike a balance between his personal and professional lives. This includes his relationships and his football career. His capacity to manage these various elements of his life speaks to his ability to plan, adapt, and show commitment to both his loved ones and his job.

In conclusion, Davante Adams's family and relationships shed light on his personality, principles, and the elements that have shaped him. His close ties to his family, his responsibilities as a father, and his community activity show that he is a well-rounded person who appreciates both his personal and professional relationships.

10.2: Off-field interests and activities

The hobbies and extracurricular pursuits of Davante Adams provide a window into his complex personality and how he spends his free time. His life revolves around football, but he also has a variety of interests outside of football that help him to be a well-rounded person.

Davante Adams

Adams is a music enthusiast who frequently communicates his musical interests to his audience. He has a history of writing, performing, and listening to music. He also occasionally shares his musical adventures on social media. His love of music gives him a creative outlet outside of football.

Fashion & Style:
Adams's sense of style is apparent both on and off the football field, as evidenced by his attire selections. He has received praise for his distinctive sense of style and has been highlighted in fashion articles. He can convey his uniqueness and personality through his passion for fashion.

Adams has demonstrated an interest in video games and esports. He has interacted with gamers' fans and peers, as well as taken part in esports-related activities. His interest in video games demonstrates his capacity to establish connections with people outside the football community.

Davante Adams

Family time is a significant part of Adams' life off the field. He values spending time with his daughter, Davante Jr., and his loved ones. He frequently posts touching memories and experiences with his family on social media, showcasing their close relationship and dedication to family values.

Community Service:
Adams' commitment to serving his community is a noteworthy off-field pursuit. He participates in charity endeavors and projects to improve the lives of people. His commitment to the community demonstrates his compassion and drive to make a real difference.

Social Concerns & Advocacy:
Adams has made use of his platform to promote social concerns and fight for constructive change. He has voiced his opinions on relevant social issues and backed programs that try to combat injustice and inequality. He is committed to making a difference, as evidenced by his determination to use his influence for good.

Davante Adams

Adams's hobbies outside of sports include travel and adventure. He has shown an interest in learning about different locations and cultures by posting snippets of his travel adventures on social media. He can relax and widen his horizons thanks to his passion for travel.

Personal Development:
Outside of football, Adams participates in activities that advance his well-being and personal development. His dedication to personal development compliments his professional accomplishments, whether it is learning new skills, leading a healthy lifestyle, or practicing self-care.

In conclusion, Davante Adams' extracurricular efforts and interests show his wide range of interests and passions. He participates in a variety of activities, from music and fashion to community service and personal development, that add to his well-rounded identity and the good influence he hopes to have both on and off the field.

CHAPTER 11: COMMUNITY INVOLVEMENT

Davante Adams' dedication to giving back to the community exemplifies his desire to have a positive influence off the football field. His efforts go beyond the game, demonstrating his kindness, leadership, and commitment to give back to the neighborhoods that have supported him.

Adams actively participates in humanitarian projects that try to better the lives of others. He collaborates with several organizations to fundraise, donate, and promote causes that are important to him. His involvement spans a variety of social issues and involves activities, initiatives, and partnerships.

Adams's connection with groups that seek to elevate and inspire young people shows that he is focused on empowering young people. He takes part in initiatives that promote education, mentoring, and wise decision-making to serve as an example for young people.

Support for underprivileged Communities:
Adams shows a dedication to aiding underprivileged communities through his humanitarian activities. He attempts to close gaps and help those in need, tackling issues with social fairness, healthcare, and education.

Engaging with Fans and Supporters:
As part of his community commitment, Adams actively interacts with his fan base and supporters. He interacts with fans, attends fan gatherings, and uses his position to raise awareness for charity issues. His interactions with his followers encourage support for several activities.

Adams utilizes his voice to promote positive change in addition to making specific philanthropic contributions. He uses his power to spread awareness about significant issues affecting communities, speaks out about social issues, fights for equality and justice, and campaigns for these causes.

Participation in Local Initiatives:
Adams's involvement with Local Initiatives is a result of his ties to his hometown and the cities where he has played. To develop worthwhile programs and opportunities for locals, he works with local businesses, schools, and community organizations.

Partnerships with Nonprofits:
Adams frequently forms alliances with well-known nonprofits and organizations as part of her commitment to the community. Through these partnerships, he may increase the effect of his work and collaborate with motivated people and organizations that share his ideals.

Adams encourages others to participate in philanthropic activities by setting an excellent example, especially other athletes and members of the public. His deeds inspire a giving mindset and serve as a reminder to others of the value of using one's position to effect change for the better.

In conclusion, Davante Adams's involvement in the community extends beyond football. He supports those in need, advocates for positive change, and uses his platform, money, and influence to assist worthwhile organizations. His passion for making a difference is a testament to his moral character, ethical principles, and desire to make a difference off the field.

11.1: Charity work

Davante Adams' dedication to charitable activities displays his sensitivity, compassion, and commitment to giving back to the community. His participation in philanthropic endeavors is a reflection of his desire to improve the lives of others and deal with numerous societal challenges.

Davante Adams

Adams Family Foundation:
To help a variety of humanitarian organizations, Davante Adams and his family founded the Adams Family Foundation. The foundation's goal is to help underprivileged people and communities by offering assistance, opportunities, and resources, with a special emphasis on social justice, education, and youth empowerment.

Youth Empowerment and Education:
Adams' charitable activity heavily emphasizes the need for youth empowerment and education. To help young people realize their full potential, he works with organizations that offer educational resources, mentorship programs, and scholarships.

Initiatives for Healthcare and Well-being:
Adams is participating in programs that support healthcare and well-being in local communities. He backs initiatives that expand access to healthcare, increase public knowledge of health issues, and promote healthy living among individuals and families.

Davante Adams

Community Outreach and Engagement:
Adams establishes direct contact with locals who are in need through community outreach and engagement. He takes part in activities that give food, supplies, and resources to underprivileged communities, demonstrating his dedication to having a real impact.

Support for Underprivileged Families:
Adams also works with underprivileged families as part of his charitable endeavors. He works with institutions that give struggling families access to necessities including food, clothing, and shelter.

Adams uses his influence to promote social justice and bring attention to structural problems that affect underprivileged populations. He uses his platform to speak out against injustice, racism, and inequality while also using his power to promote change.

Positive Change Inspiration:

Davante Adams

Adams motivates others to get involved and make a difference through his charitable activity. His deeds set an example for athletes, followers, and the broader public, fostering a spirit of altruism and using one's power for the common good.

Collaborations with Partners:
To increase the impact of his charitable activities, Adams works with corporate partners, fellow athletes, and nonprofit groups. Through these partnerships, he can make the most of his resources and reach a larger audience, increasing the benefits of his work.

Adams' dedication to charitable activity goes above and beyond money contributions. He commits his time, energy, and personal commitment to several projects, displaying his hands-on approach to making a significant difference.

In conclusion, Davante Adams' charitable work demonstrates his commitment to enhancing other people's lives and solving important social challenges.

Davante Adams

He demonstrates his commitment to using his position for good change and leaving a long-lasting legacy of kindness and community support through his foundation, partnerships, and personal involvement.

11.2: Community Engagement

Davante Adams's community involvement activities span a wider range of interactions and projects that link him with supporters, locals, and organizations in the communities he belongs to. These activities go beyond charitable work. His dedication to volunteer work in the community is a reflection of his desire to have a good influence and forge enduring bonds outside of football.

Adams constantly interacts with his followers on social media and at public gatherings. In addition to sharing updates about his life and career, he answers fan letters and expresses gratitude for the support he has received. He feels connected to his supporters because of this one-on-one relationship.

Davante Adams

Meet-and-Greets and Fan Events:
Adams takes part in meet-and-greets, fan events, and autograph sessions. Fans have the chance to engage with him in person, take pictures with him, and make lifelong memories through these encounters. His popularity and good relationships with fans are a result of his approachability and eagerness to interact.

Adams hosts youth clinics, workshops, and sporting activities in his capacity as a role model for young athletes. These events give ambitious athletes the ability to learn from them, get coaching advice, and obtain insightful knowledge about their path to the NFL.

.

Visits, presentations, and educational activities are all part of Adams' involvement with schools. In his motivational talks, he stresses the value of education and exhorts students to pursue their goals on and off the field.

Adams takes part in community initiatives and events that are put up by area businesses, schools, and organizations. His presence offers value and raises awareness for significant causes, whether it's a charity event, a local festival, or a campaign.

Collaboration with Local Businesses:
To assist community involvement initiatives, Adams frequently works with local businesses. He might show up at events like store openings, sales, or promotions, enhancing the local business climate and strengthening ties within the neighborhood.

Participation in Team-Organised Initiatives: Adams participates in Team-Organised Community Initiatives as a member of the Green Bay Packers. These could consist of volunteer work, outreach initiatives, and activities that put participants in contact with the neighborhood's population.

Spreading Encouragement and Positivity: Adams's upbeat attitude and inspirational messages support his community participation initiatives. He encourages everyone around him to strive for their best by spreading words of inspiration, optimism, and unity through his platform.

Advocacy & Social Change:
Adams uses his position to promote social change and justice outside of his involvement in athletics. He might take part in protests, awareness drives, and other activities meant to address societal problems and effect constructive change.

In conclusion, Davante Adams's involvement in the community includes a range of conversations, activities, and projects that link him with supporters, groups, and locals. His influence off the football field and his reputation as a good role model are largely due to his approachability, influence, and commitment to making a difference.

CHAPTER 12: LEGACY AND IMPACT

The legacy and influence of Davante Adams go far beyond his football-related accomplishments. The impact of his contributions to the game, his community, and his role as a good role model will be felt for many years to come.

Adams's incredible skill, reliability, and capacity to reimagine the receiver position are what define his on-field legacy. He has been a key contributor to the Packers' success, holding numerous league and franchise records, and has been chosen for the Pro Bowl. His dominance and influence on the game solidify his reputation as one of the greatest wide receivers in NFL history.

Davante Adams

Contributions to the Packers:
There is no disputing Adams' influence on the Green
Bay Packers. During his tenure, he has been a vital factor
in the team's offensive performance, a prime target for
top quarterbacks like Aaron Rodgers, and a pillar of
consistency. The Packers' winning culture has been
influenced by his leadership and capacity to improve
people around him.

Impact on the Community:
Adams's dedication to volunteer work and humanitarian
endeavors has a long-lasting influence on the lives of
numerous others. He has impacted underserved
communities, empowered youngsters, and sparked
positive change through his foundation, partnerships, and
personal initiatives. Beyond football, his support for
social justice increases the scope of his influence.

Adams is a role model for aspiring athletes as well as a
source of inspiration for both fans and everyday people.
His rise from obscurity to NFL stardom is a testament to
the effectiveness of perseverance, hard effort, and

fortitude. He serves as an example of how hard effort and commitment may lead to success.

Adams uses his platform to speak out for social change and tackle pressing causes, so his voice goes beyond the football field. His determination to have a constructive influence on society is demonstrated by his readiness to speak out against injustice and inequity.

Positive Representation:
As a professional athlete, Adams sets a good example for others with his morals and conduct. He is the epitome of good sportsmanship, humility, and genuine gratitude for his followers and fans. He promotes the sport in a way that upholds its integrity and enhances its reputation.

Community Engagement:
Adams' involvement in the Green Bay area and beyond goes beyond his position as a player. He interacts with followers, takes part in neighborhood activities, and continues to be woven into the fabric of the towns he has lived in.

Continued Influence:

As Adams's career progresses, his legacy will continue to have an impact on social issues, football, and the lives he touches through his charitable efforts. His influence on the sport and society will continue long after his playing career is over.

In conclusion, Davante Adams' legacy and impact include his on-field accomplishments, his services to the community, and his function as an agent of change. His legacy will be defined by his football prowess and dedication to making a difference, guaranteeing that his influence will last long after his playing days are finished.

12.1: Influence on the game of football

Football player Davante Adams has a significant impact on the sport that goes beyond his achievements and affects the entire landscape of the game. His performance, work ethic, and contributions have influenced how wide receivers are seen and utilized.

Davante Adams

Adams' distinctive playing style has changed what is expected of a wide receiver in the current era, redefining the wide receiver position. To create separation and make challenging catches, he combines excellent route-running, deft footwork, and a large catch radius. He has raised the bar for the position with his versatility as an inside and outside receiver.

Route-Running Accuracy:
Adams is regarded as one of the league's top route-runners. His capacity to sell routes, shift directions with ease, and establish separation has come to define his style of play. Adams is looked to as a role model by younger players and aspiring receivers to master this vital ability.

Adams's aptitude for getting considerable yardage after the catch (YAC) demonstrates his elusiveness and ability to turn brief receptions into significant gains. His YAC prowess has influenced how teams use short passing plays as a complement to the rushing attack.

Davante Adams

Chemistry with Quarterbacks:
Adams's close relationship and chemistry with his quarterbacks, especially Aaron Rodgers, serve as a reminder of the importance of having a solid rapport with your quarterback. For other receiver-quarterback pairings, his ability to anticipate throws, adapt to improvised plays, and execute timing routes has served as an example.

Physicality and Red Zone Dominance:
Teams' use of tall, physical receivers has changed as a result of Adams' success in contested catches in red zone situations. His ability to successfully shield defenders with his body and prevail in one-on-one matches in crucial circumstances has caused the league to place more attention on receiving attributes with a similar skill set.

Adams's continuous capacity for game-changing performances has brought attention to the value of having a dependable and dynamic playmaker on a team's squad. His dependability during crucial downs, in constrained circumstances, and crucial scenarios has evolved into a template for receivers aiming to be their team's go-to target.

Influence on Young People and Future Players:
Future football players are inspired by Adams's transformation from an unnoticed high school recruit to an NFL superstar. He is looked up to by young athletes and receivers as an illustration of how perseverance, hard effort, and dedication can result in success at the highest level.

Versatility and Adaptability:
Adams' success at both the outside and slot positions demonstrates the value of having a wide receiver with a diverse skill set. Teams now use receivers differently to take advantage of defensive matchups thanks to his versatility to various offensive schemes and positions.

In conclusion, Davante Adams' impact on football transcends honors and statistics. His performance, abilities, and influence on how the wide receiver position is viewed have left a long-lasting imprint on the game. He has established a new bar for excellence, motivating present and upcoming players to step up their play and rethink what it takes to be a premier wide receiver.

12.2: Contributions to the team:

Davante Adams has made significant and far-reaching contributions to the Green Bay Packers as well as the game of football as a whole. His on-field prowess, leadership, and commitment to enhancing the game have made a lasting impression on both levels.

Efforts on behalf of the Green Bay Packers:

1. Offensive Anchor: The Packers' offense has been anchored by Adams. His dependable top-tier receiving performance has given the team's passing game stability and dependability.

2. Go-To Target: Adams is a quarterback's go-to target because of his propensity to make big catches in crunch

time, especially for Aaron Rodgers. His presence gives the offense a dependable means of making significant gains and moving the chains.

3. Dominance in the Red Zone: The Packers' efficiency in scoring has been greatly impacted by Adams' skill in the red zone. He has made many contested catches and found gaps, which has resulted in many scores and helped the team win.

4. Leadership and Mentorship: As an experienced player, Adams has acted as a mentor to younger players both on and off the field. His dedication, readiness, and upbeat demeanor served as role models for his coworkers and promoted an excellence-oriented environment.

5. Locker Room Presence: Adams's character and fellow comradery have boosted team chemistry and cohesion. The Packers' entire dynamic is improved by his pleasant interactions and capacity to connect with players in every position.

12.3: Contributions to the Sport

1. Redefining Receiver Play:

The way receivers handle contested catches, separation methods, and route running has been inspired by Adams' playing style. For aspiring wide receivers, his footwork, agility, and physicality have become models.

2. Route-Running Emphasis:

Adams' outstanding route-running abilities have brought attention to how crucial accuracy is in this area of the game. His expertise with route intricacies and capacity for separation has turned into a teaching and development focus.

3. Yards After Catch (YAC) Emphasis:

Adams' capacity to gain big yardage after the catch highlights the significance of this element of offensive strategy. His accomplishments have inspired clubs to use short-passing plays that let receivers demonstrate their elusiveness.

4. Wide Receiver-QB Chemistry:

Davante Adams

Adams's relationship with his quarterbacks demonstrates the importance of wide receivers and their quarterbacks building chemistry. He has established a benchmark for the cooperation between pass catchers and passers thanks to his ability to anticipate throws and adapt to various quarterbacks.

5. Motivation for Young Athletes:
Adams' transformation from an under-recruited high school player to an NFL superstar serves as motivation for young athletes. His experience serves as proof that perseverance, hard effort, and determination may result in extraordinary achievement.

6. Social Justice Advocacy:
Adams's use of his position to promote social justice and constructive change exemplifies the part that athletes may play in resolving significant societal problems. His activism serves as an example of the wider influence sportsmen can have outside of their sport.

Davante Adams

In conclusion, Davante Adams has made contributions to the Green Bay Packers and the game of football that go above and beyond his numbers. He serves as an example for aspiring sportsmen and other professionals because of his impact on his team's performance, his impact on receiver play, and his dedication to making changes for the better. His legacy is one of excellence, leadership, and using one's position to advance society and the game.

Davante Adams

CHAPTER 13: FUTURE GOALS AND ASPIRATIONS

The Green Bay Packers' incredibly gifted wide receiver Davante Adams has had a successful start to his NFL career. He surely has future objectives and aspirations, though, just like any ambitious athlete, which he intends to realize.

1. Winning the Super Bowl:
Adams' top goal is unquestionably to become a Super Bowl champion. Adams, who has played a significant role in the Packers' success over several seasons, has repeatedly displayed his talent and tenacity. He would join the NFL's elite with a Super Bowl victory, which would also confirm his unceasing efforts and unwavering devotion to the sport.

2. Consistently Earning All-Pro and Pro Bowl Honors:
In recent years, Adams has received back-to-back
All-Pro and Pro Bowl selections, which is already
recognized for his exceptional accomplishments. His
objective is probably to remain a dominant force in the
league and to routinely win these awards every year.
Adams aspires to be regarded as one of the greatest wide
receivers in NFL history, and being consistently praised
for his outstanding on-field performance would
encourage him to achieve this goal.

3. Breaking NFL and Franchise Records:
Adams has the opportunity to leave his mark on history
thanks to his extraordinary talent and friendship with
Packers quarterback Aaron Rodgers. Adams has his eyes
set on breaking several franchise records established by
illustrious Packers receivers like Don Hutson and Jordy
Nelson. Additionally, setting NFL records would raise
his legacy and further cement his place in football
history. Adams surely wants to break league records in

all areas of receiving, whether it's for a single season or receptions, touchdowns, or yardage.

4. Creating a Charitable Legacy:
Outside of football, Adams has demonstrated a desire to have a beneficial influence on the neighborhood. Throughout his career, he has participated in a wide range of humanitarian endeavors, frequently giving his time and money to aid those in need. Adams wants to leave a lasting charity legacy that endures after his playing career. He wants to have a beneficial impact on people's lives and encourage future generations to follow in his footsteps, whether through his foundation or collaborations with already-established organizations.

5. Longevity and Success
Throughout His Career: Adams is aware of the value of having a long NFL career and aspires to have a fruitful and successful one that lasts for many seasons. He could accomplish his other objectives and solidify his status as one of the best wide receivers in game history if he could

play with consistency, stay healthy, and produce at a high level for a sustained period.

Davante Adams has high expectations for his future in the NFL, to sum up. He aspires to winning the Super Bowl, earning continued acclaim by being named to the All-Pro and Pro Bowl teams, shattering franchise and NFL records, leaving a charitable legacy, and enjoying a lengthy, fruitful career. Adams can make these dreams come true and make a lasting impact on both the sport and his community with his abilities, commitment, and desire.

13.1: Anticipated contributions to the sport

One of the best wide receivers in the National Football League (NFL), Davante Adams is respected for his great abilities, adaptable playing style, and exceptional football knowledge. His planned contributions to the sport are therefore anticipated to be substantial and influential. Here are some specifics on how Adams is prepared to impact football:

1. Outstanding Route Running:
Davante Adams has earned a reputation as one of the NFL's top route runners. He has an amazing talent for getting away from opponents by making quick cutbacks, using deft feet, and making subtle motions. Adams is a continuous threat to opposing secondaries thanks to his route-running prowess, which allows him to continually find openings in opposing defenses. He excels at a variety of routes, including slants, dig routes, and deep routes.

2. Reliable Hands:
Adams' capacity to catch nearly anything thrown his way is undoubtedly one of his finest assets. He rarely drops catchable passes and is renowned for his excellent attention and strong hands. Adams can make difficult grabs in crowded or challenging conditions thanks to his superb hand-eye coordination. His dependability as a pass-catcher not only improves his stats but also offers

his quarterback a safety net, making him a go-to target in game-changing circumstances.

3. Tremendous Playmaking:

Adams is a tremendous playmaker thanks to his unusual combination of accurate route running and powerful athleticism. He frequently uses his tremendous speed and after-catch acceleration to turn short passes into long gains. Adams' dexterity and mobility allow him to avoid opponents and break tackles, frequently converting ordinary plays into thrilling touchdowns or game-changing plays.

4. Red Zone Dominance:

Adams is a force to be reckoned with in the red zone thanks to his 6'1" height and exceptional leaping abilities. When the field closes in, quarterbacks will be able to easily target him because of his natural ability to create separation and good hands. Adams' commanding presence necessitates double coverage, frequently creating mismatches elsewhere on the field that help his team by creating openings for his teammates.

Davante Adams

5. Leadership and Work Ethic:
Adams' contributions to the game go beyond his performance on the field. He enjoys high regard from both his teammates and coaches due to his excellent work ethic, commitment, and leadership qualities. His eagerness to mentor younger players and dedication to honing his trade serve as an example for the squad as a whole. Adams is a wonderful addition to any club he represents because of the way he leads, both on and off the field.

In conclusion, Davante Adams will undoubtedly make a significant impact on the game of football. He has made a name for himself as one of the NFL's most formidable wide receivers thanks to his excellent route running, trustworthy hands, explosive playmaking, dominance in the red zone, and leadership abilities. Expect him to carry on having such a remarkable influence, enhancing the offensive of his team and encouraging those around him for years to come.

CONCLUSION

A fascinating and enlightening journey through the life, career, and effect of one of the NFL's most dynamic and significant players. Readers have been given a behind-the-scenes glimpse into the life of a young man who, despite all odds, converted himself into a football phenomenon and a beacon of greatness through the pages of this book.

Adams' journey from obscurity to prominence as a top-tier NFL wide receiver is one of unrelenting tenacity, unflinching passion, and unwavering dedication. The story has shed light on the crucial occasions, difficulties, and victories that helped him become the outstanding athlete and person he is today. His rise from a little-known high school player to a record-breaking NFL great exemplifies the value of tenacity and each person's capacity to overcome challenges.

Davante Adams

The book delves into the many facets of Adams' personality, examining not only his physical talent but also his strong sense of family, his contributions to his community, and his resolve to use his platform for good. The man behind the jersey has been revealed to readers on these pages; he is a caring father, a tireless fighter for the underdog, and a role model for numerous fans and aspiring athletes.

The book "Davante Adams: Redefining Receiver Dominance" skillfully details his meteoric ascent to fame, his illustrious accomplishments, and his never-ending mission to reinvent the receiver position. His excellent on-field abilities, including his route-running accuracy and his capacity for clutch receptions in pressure situations, have been highlighted in the story. Beyond the numbers, the book also highlights his impact on football, his enduring influence on the Green Bay Packers, and his persistent commitment to becoming a force for good in the wider world of sports.

Davante Adams

The concluding chapter of this gripping book leaves readers with a profound understanding of the transformational power of commitment, tenacity, and the pursuit of excellence. The life of Davante Adams is a tribute to the potential that resides within every person. It serves as a reminder that through perseverance, hard work, and the adoption of the correct attitude, it is possible to surpass expectations and redefine what it means to be a dominant force both on and off the field.

"Davante Adams: Redefining Receiver Dominance" is more than simply a football narrative; it's also about overcoming hardship, the enduring value of family and community, and the power to effect change for the better. It is a story that appeals to sports fans, aspiring athletes, and everyone looking for evidence of the immense potential that each of us possesses.

Made in United States
Troutdale, OR
11/28/2023